20 Hill Walks

Glen Coe
and
Lochaber

R U A R I D H P R I N G L E

Series Editor: Roger Smith

EDINBURGH: THE STATIONERY OFFICE

Acknowledgements

Thanks are due to the following for their kind help: Derrick
Warner of the National Trust for Scotland for the use of the
resources at Achnacon and for being a fountain of knowledge,
contacts, useful suggestions, and general help; Mark Bates of
Heritage Woodlands for numerous acts of botanical clarification;
Ian Fraser of The University of Edinburgh Placename Survey and
Archive for help with placenames; Simon Harley of Edinburgh
University Geology Department for freely-given guidance on
matters igneous; Fort William Tourist Information Centre and
West Highland Estates for valuable information; Michael Newton
for advice on Gaelic and Highland history; Varda Hood for good
company in atrocious weather, and being a packhorse after my
operation; Wendy Pringle for offers of transport; and Kari Williams,
for much appreciated physio-therapeutic bullying.

Finally, special thanks to Cameron McNeish and Roger Smith,
without whom none of this would have been possible.

ISBN 0 11 495806 8

Contents

USEFUL INFORMATION

The length of each walk is given in kilometres and miles, but in the text measurements of distance are metric for simplicity. However, the traditional classification of Scotland's mountains into 'Munros' (mountains of 3000 feet or over) and 'Corbetts' (mountains of 2500 to 2999 feet) uses imperial measurements. A whole industry has formed around this classification, which becomes esoteric in conversion to metric; so major heights are given in both feet and metres.

The Munro phenomenon began when Sir Hugh Munro published his *Tables of Heights Over 3000 Feet* in 1891: the first proper survey of Scotland's highest peaks. These he subdivided into separate mountains, which became known as 'Munros'; and subsidiary summits, or 'Tops'. The list of 'Munroists' (people who have climbed all 284 Munros) is fast approaching 2000. The 'Corbetts', first collated by John Rooke Corbett in a list which was not published until after his death, are also increasingly popular. The maps in this book use the following symbols to indicate summit classification:

▲ - Munros; △ - Tops; ● - Corbetts; ○ - hills below 2499 feet.

Conversion Factors

to convert: **miles** to **kilometres**   divide by **1.6093**
                kilometres to **miles**   multiply by **0.6214**
                feet to **metres**   divide by **0.3048**
                metres to **feet**   multiply by **3.281**

Times

Times for walks are not given as they can be misleading. An approximation for an average person can be calculated using Naismith's Rule, which takes as its basis an average walking speed of 5kph, to which it adds 30 minutes for every 300m of ascent. For Naismith's Rule to be accurate, it should be adapted using personal estimates of walking speeds.

Gaelic

Most hill and place names in the Highlands are in Gaelic (pronounced '**ga**-lic' not '**gay**-lic'); the universal language until the comparatively recent ingress of English. Knowledge of their meaning and pronunciation is a great aid to understanding and enjoyment of the area, as such names are often historically and

Opposite: Aonach Dubh above Loch Achtriochtan, Glencoe.

geographically highly informative, yet present a potential
communications barrier. Many have become anglicised (e.g. Ben
Nevis), and often meanings have become obscured by spelling
inaccuracies dating from early cartographical surveys. Where
possible, an English translation is given for prominent names, along
with their pronunciation.

An initial stumbling block for many people is that written Gaelic
represents sounds in ways different from English; partly because the
language covers sounds which often simply have no direct English
equivalent, using only 18 letters. The phonetic pronunciations
given can therefore only be approximations, but should at least
enable comprehension by a Gaelic speaker.

Main points to note: the sound of consonants followed by an 'h' is
changed (e.g. 'bh' and 'mh' sound like the English 'v'); 'ch' is a
sound made with the back of the throat (as in 'loch'); and 't's and
'd's sound thicker than in English (try putting the tip of the
tongue behind the lower teeth). In certain situations, 'n' and 'l'
have a following small nasal 'yu' sound, like the 'n' in 'new'. In the
pronunciations given, this is indicated by a 'y', while bold type
indicates a stressed syllable, a colon indicates a lengthening of the
preceding vowel, and a hyphen is used to separate syllables where
confusion is possible. *Scottish Hill and Mountain Names* by Peter
Drummond (Scottish Mountaineering Trust, 1991) is recommended as further reading.

Some Common Terms

Allt (owlt). A burn or stream.
Abhainn (av**Yn**ʸ). A river.
Aonach (**eo**:noch) A ridge.
Baile (**ba**la) A town.
Bealach (**bya**loch). Originally a pass, but in hillwalking
        terminology commonly refers to a col or saddle.
Beinn (bʸn). A mountain. Anglicised to the familiar *ben*.
Bothy. From the Gaelic *bothain* (**baw**an): a cottage or
        hut. Now generally refers to a building
        providing open shelter.
Càrn (kaarn). A cairn, but can also refer to a mountain
        with a conical form.
Coille (**col**ya). A wood.
Coire (**kor**a). Anglicised to *corrie*: a bowl shaped glacial
        hollow.
Doire (**dor**a). A copse or wood.
Gleann (glyown). Anglicised to glen: a (relatively) steep-
        sided valley.

Lochain (**loch**Yn^y). A little loch (ie. lake). Often anglicised to *lochan*.

Sgùrr (skoor) or **Sgòr(r)** (skor). A sharp peak.

Shieling. A homestead. Originally a northern English word, its west coast Gaelic equivalent is *ruighe* (**roo**ee).

Stob (stob). A jutting peak.

Tourist Information

The main information source for the area is the Fort William Tourist Information Centre in Cameron Square (01397 703781), which is open all year. Local centres at Spean Bridge (01397 712576) and Ballachulish (01855 811296) are open from Easter to October. Information on the Glen Coe area can be obtained at the National Trust for Scotland Visitor Centre (01855 811307) on the A82 south of the Clachaig Inn. This centre is soon to be moved to a new site at the campsite on the A82, 1.5km south-east of Glencoe village.

Public Transport

The area is reasonably well served with public transport, and walkers are encouraged to use this wherever possible. Some useful telephone numbers are: Scottish Citylink (includes Skye-Ways coaches) – 0141 332 9644; British Rail – 0345 484950; Gaelicbus – 01855 811229; Highland Bus & Coach – 01463 239292; the Post Office (for Post Buses) – 01463 256273. Timetable information is usually available from Tourist Information Centres.

Fort William is a node for coach routes (Scottish Citylink) from Glasgow (stopping at Bridge of Orchy, the Kingshouse, Glencoe, Ballachulish), Aviemore (stopping at Roybridge, Glen Spean), Inverness, and Skye. There are regular trains (including a sleeper service) from Glasgow to Fort William and onwards to Mallaig, stopping at Bridge of Orchy, Rannoch, Corrour, Tulloch, Roybridge and Spean Bridge. This, the West Highland Line, is one of the world's most beautiful railway journeys, and worth a trip in itself.

Local buses serve the main towns and villages of the area. There are services between Fort William and Glencoe (Scottish Citylink and Gaelicbus), Kinlochleven (Gaelicbus), Glen Nevis (Gaelicbus), and Roy Bridge (Highland Bus & Coach). Post buses provide links to the smaller communities, and will connect with trains and buses: very useful for reaching remoter parts such as Glen Etive and Victoria Bridge (Forest Lodge).

Accommodation

Hotels/Guesthouses/Bed & Breakfast: Roybridge, Spean Bridge, Fort William, Onich, Kentallen, North Ballachulish, Kinlochleven, Kingshouse, Clachaig, Glencoe village, Glen Coe, Ballachulish, Duror, Inveroran, Bridge of Orchy, and Rannoch station. A 'Book-a-Bed-Ahead' service is available through all Tourist Information Centres.

Self catering: Roybridge, Spean Bridge, Fort William, Corran, Onich, Ballachulish, Kinlochleven, Mamore Lodge (Kinlochmore), Kentallen, Glencoe village and Glen Coe.

Hostels and bunkhouses: Auchlauchrach (near Roybridge) – Aite Cruinnichidh Backpackers Lodge (01397 712 315); Glen Nevis – Ben Nevis Bunkhouse (01397 702240) and Glen Nevis Youth Hostel (01397 702336); Fort William – Fort William Backpackers (01397 700711); Corpach – The Smiddy Bunkhouse (01397 772467); Inchree (near Onich) – Inchree Bunkhouse (01855 821287); Glen Coe – Glencoe Youth Hostel (01855 811219), Leacantuim Farm Bunkhouses (01855 811256); Bridge of Orchy – Bridge of Orchy Hotel Bunkhouse (01838 400208); and Corrour station - Morgan's Den (01397 732236).

Climbers' huts: Steall, Glen Nevis (Lochaber Mountaineering Club); CIC Hut, Ben Nevis (Scottish Mountaineering Club, usually booked months in advance); Onich (Lomond Mountaineering Club, Mountaineering Council of Scotland); Kinlochleven (Fell & Rock Climbing Club); Lagangarbh (Scottish Mountaineering Club); Glen Etive – Inbhir-fhaolain (Grampian Club) and The Smiddy (Forventure Trust); Blackrock Cottage, White Corries (Ladies Scottish Climbing Club); Clashgour schoolhouse near Loch Tulla (Glasgow University Mountaineering Club).

Campsites: Roybridge, Glen Nevis, Caolasnacon (Loch Leven), Invercoe, Leacantuim, A82 1.5km south-east of Glencoe village. Camping is also tolerated north of the river by the Kingshouse.

Enjoying the Mountains

The Highland landscape is not a wilderness in the true sense: most is privately owned in the form of large estates, and provides local income and employment. Despite a centuries-old tradition of a moral 'right to roam', walkers presently have no legal right of access to hill-country. Some historically well-used paths are legally enshrined 'public rights of way', which members of the public have a right to use at any time – but elsewhere, anyone who goes onto land without the consent of the landowner is technically a 'trespasser'. Trespass is not itself a criminal offence and no prosecution can follow unless actual damage has been caused, a trespasser can be asked to leave, and removed using 'reasonable force' (whatever that is!) should he or she refuse. Riding a bicycle along a footpath in the absence of a specific right to do so (e.g. the presence of a public right of way) is an offence.

The result of Scottish law's inherent ambiguity on this subject has been that walking on private land is generally tolerated: a fragile tradition based upon mutual compromise and respect, and consideration for estate needs.

The primary activities affecting the area covered by this book are deer stalking (ie. hunting), sheep rearing and grouse shooting. Yearly culls of red deer (whose natural predators have been made extinct) are vital to prevent the landscape becoming a wasteland through overgrazing. The lambing season is between March and May. During this time particularly, disturbance to sheep should be avoided, and dogs kept out of lambing areas. The grouse shooting season runs from 12 August to 10 December.

Deer stalking generally takes place from 1 July to 20 October, when the shooting of stags ends, although hinds may be culled until 15 February. **The critical time is from mid August or early September to mid October,** during which days of work can be destroyed by walkers scattering unseen deer. Telephone numbers given at the start of relevant chapters under the heading **Stalking Information** can be used to check that walks planned during this period pose no problem, and to plan alternatives if necessary. Estate staff are usually extremely helpful. but even if faced with an obstructive response, be flexible. Some landowners (NTS –the National Trust for Scotland – for example) welcome hillwalkers at any time, and walking is always possible somewhere. Anyone with serious access concerns could perhaps report them to the Access Officer of the Mountaineering Council of Scotland (4a St Catherine's Road, Perth PH1 5SE).

A 'Concordat on Access' has been prepared by a forum of interested parties, including landowners, local authorities, and mountaineering, walking and conservation bodies, providing for the first time a mutually agreed framework of conduct for all hill users. This is available from the Mountaineering Council of Scotland. Recommended reading: *Heading for the Scottish Hills*, published by the Scottish Mountaineering Trust.

Looking after the Mountain Environment

Erosion
The book covers an area that is one of the most popular in the Highlands for hillwalking, yet is also one of the wettest, and hence prone to rapid erosion. As visitor numbers increase, many of the paths which have formed along most ridges and popular routes are

degenerating. Repair work is being done, but much is voluntary, some find the results intrusive, and the problem expands as fast as its symptoms are treated.

Treading lightly

Paths erode because feet destroy the soil's structure, allowing rainfall to wash it away. For minimal impact always follow existing paths where possible – even when they are wet and muddy, and avoid walking along the edges of paths to avoid boggy sections, as this rapidly widens them (especially during or soon after wet spells, when the soil is most easily damaged). Anyone really worried about wet feet could try jumping in the first stream encountered. This removes any need to avoid wet areas – reducing erosion and making far more carefree! Rock or stones are obviously tougher than vegetation or soil, so walk on them where possible.

Cairns

Increasing traffic has also led to a proliferation of cairns. These reduce wildness, promote erosion by the removal of stones from their surroundings, disrupt plant communities, reduce wildlife cover, and cause navigational confusion (maybe not for you, but for someone else). As a result, indiscriminate cairn building is widely frowned upon (the NTS strongly discourages it on their properties), and the dismantling of cairns is encouraged – *provided* they have no cultural or archaeological significance (see for example Walk 13). Lichen-free upper stone surfaces usually suggest a cairn is recent. In vegetated areas especially, stones should ideally be replaced in their original holes, lichen-side up.

Bicycles

The use of all-terrain bicycles is generally accepted on bulldozed tracks, but on footpaths and open country their use accelerates erosion (particularly when the ground is wet after rain), and for this reason bicycles should not be used in such areas.

Answering nature's call

The number of visitors answering 'calls of nature' in wild areas is an increasing problem, with effects ranging from reduced enjoyment to pollution of streamwater and the risk of illness. Only go to the toilet 200m or more from a water source or path, and either carry a lighter to burn used toilet roll (but only when this poses no fire risk) or (when possible!) use stones or vegetation instead. Ideally carry a trowel and bury what you leave behind (lightweight folding trowels are available for this purpose).

Litter

Don't leave litter – even biodegradable leftovers such as orange peel and apple cores, as these attract scavenging birds which wreak havoc on upland bird populations during the nesting season. Pocketing other people's dropped wrappers etc. for disposal later is a very good habit to get into.

Safety

The routes in this book are described predominantly for summer conditions. All are at least as good under snow, but in such conditions the Scottish peaks become much more serious, requiring full mountaineering skills. In wintry conditions, crampons and an ice-axe, and practice using them, are mandatory, and navigational skills must be finely honed.

Even in summer, most routes described are potentially serious, and are intended only for properly equipped hillwalkers who can navigate competently on high mountains in foul weather and low visibility. Blizzards, sub-zero temperatures and gale force winds occur on Scotland's mountains throughout the year, often with little warning, and rain and low cloud (as those familiar with the area covered by this book will be all too aware!) often seem the rule rather than the exception. Those lacking the necessary experience should accompany someone who has it, or attend one of the excellent courses available from recognised outdoor centres.

Midges and Ticks

First-time visitors to the area covered by this book should be aware of two blood-sucking beasts in particular. The first is the ferocious Highland Midge (Culicoides impunctatus – or, in Gaelic, *meanbh chuileag*: tiny fly). Sunlight and a breeze keep them at bay, but in dull, still conditions especially their biting swarms quickly become unbearable for the unprepared. In such conditions either keep moving, or wear a cocoon of clothes and use a repellant (those containing DEET work best). A midge-hood is a sound investment.

The second are ticks. These mites, which favour areas of bracken, insert a lance deep into the skin, often hiding in awkward places while swelling slowly from pin-head size to (given the chance) a blood-filled bag 4mm long. Care should be taken in their removal: the lance can break off, causing infection. They also occasionally transmit Lyme's disease, a bacterial infection which causes joint inflammation and arthritic problems if not treated early by antibiotics, and whose tell-tale sign is a red ring around the bite. The best defence against ticks is tucking trousers into socks or gaiters, followed by a thorough body check after a day's walking.

Introduction

The walks described in this book explore the stumps of a vanished ancient mountain range which was once as high as the Himalaya. These have been folded, fractured, stretched, heated, parched, buried, torn apart, subjected to periods of violent volcanic activity and intense glacial erosion, and have generally endured a pretty torrid time.

Fortunately for us, this has resulted in one of the most geologically and scenically fascinating landscapes in the world. From the huge volcanic cliffs of Ben Nevis and the fertile schists and shattered quartzite of the Grey Corries and Mamores to the entertainingly weathered arête of the Aonach Eagach; from the hidden cliff-girt hanging valleys of Bidean nam Bian to the graceful granite ridges of Ben Starav above the wind-ruffled salt waters of Loch Etive; and from the splendour of Buachaille Etive Mòr to the wild corries of Stob Ghabhar, the sheer scenic variety is remarkable.

In more recent times, the landscape was shaped by, and helped to shape, a long and rich yet often violent and tragic history. Evidence of human settlement and conflict accompany the walker through most of this book, even in the vast empty spaces of the once forested Rannoch Moor. After centuries of relative prosperity, the land emptied of people as huge numbers were forced to emigrate to the Lowlands or overseas colonial lands.

The underlying cause was overpopulation and impending starvation, originating in the undermining of the originally democratic clan system, and exacerbated enormously by the repercussions of the disastrous 1745-46 Jacobite rebellion. Many were forcibly evicted with great brutality for failure to meet extortionate rents, or to make way for sheep – which, along with the red deer which rule most of the area covered by this book, continue to play a major role in shaping the landscape.

For walkers, it is hillwalking and scrambling at which the area excels, although many mountain approaches are as interesting as the mountains themselves. This is reflected in the choice of routes described, which range from the 6km (3.5 mile) ascent of the little Pap of Glencoe to the challenge of Aonach Eagach's arêtes and pinnacles and the demanding traverse of the Western Mamores. One low-level walk has been included: the crossing of Rannoch Moor, without which no walking guide to the area would be complete.

With so much scope, a guide must inevitably be selective, and some may not agree with my choice of routes. However, the aim of this book is not to be exhaustive, but rather to provide a framework for exploring, and to inspire further exploration while fostering an appreciation of the rich underlying geological, natural and historical tapestry which has made the landscape what it is today.

Researching this book has given me a new insight into an area I thought, perhaps conceitedly, that I knew; revealing details and depths I was previously only superficially aware of. I could happily spend weeks on end prowling its hidden corries and wooded ravines; sitting amongst the tumbled stones of old shielings and trying to imagine the views as their not so recently departed inhabitants saw them. Far from dulling my view, intensive exposure has, for me, amplified the area's delights; some of which I hope this book will allow me to share with you.

RUARIDH PRINGLE

Opposite: Sunlight on Loch Eilde Mor.

WALK 1

BEN NEVIS BY LEDGE ROUTE
AND THE CÀRN MÒR DEARG ARÊTE

Distance: 17km (10.5 miles).
Ascent: 1560m (5100ft).
Start/finish: Lay-by west of golf club (GR135763), on A82 6km (4 miles) north of Fort William.
Maps: OS Landranger 41 *Ben Nevis, Fort William & surrounding area* or Outdoor Leisure 38 *Ben Nevis & Glencoe* or Pathfinder 277 *Ben Nevis & Fort William.* Harveys Walker's Map or Superwalker *Ben Nevis.*
Terrain: These are expeditions which should not be underestimated. The Càrn Mòr Dearg Arête provides easy and largely escapable but sometimes exposed scrambling. Though strewn with paths and navigational aids, the summit of Ben Nevis can be a serious place in poor conditions, especially if there is snow. The Ledge Route option is a scramble through spectacular cliff scenery. Though moderate technically, it demands respect and confident routefinding. Winter climbing on Ben Nevis frequently persists well into June, so prepare to encounter snow patches at least until July.
Stalking information: No problems with access at any time of year.

Gaelic names

Allt a' Mhuilinn (owlt a **voo**leen**ʸ**): Stream of the mill.
Càrn Beag Dearg (kaarn bayk **dye**rak): Little red cairn.
Càrn Dearg Meadhonach (kaarn dyerak **mee**anoch): Middle red cairn.
Càrn Mòr Dearg (kaarn moa:r **dye**rak): Big red cairn.
An Steall (an **shtyowl**): The spout.
Càrn Dearg (kaarn **dye**rak): Red cairn.
Coire Leis (kora **lays**h): Leeward corrie.
Lochan Meall an t' Suidhe (lochan myowl an **too**ya): Lochan of the mound of the seat.

Top: Ben Nevis and Càrn Mòr Dearg from Stob Coire a'Chairn to the south.

It is a mountain of superlatives. Climbers know it simply as *The* Ben. At 1344m (4406ft) Ben Nevis is not only the highest mountain in the British Isles, but a strong contender for the most spectacular, with the biggest cliffs and the longest unbroken hillside. The origin of the name is obscure, the commonly accepted derivation being the Gaelic *nibheis*, meaning venomous – a description many may feel is apt. Rising abruptly from sea-level into the prevailing moist south-westerly airflow, Ben Nevis also enjoys a reputation for the worst weather, with reported means of 300 cloud-bound days and 261 gales a year, and winds regularly exceeding 160kph. With a sub-zero mean annual summit temperature, huge levels of precipitation – which can fall as snow at any time of year – ensure that snow disappears from beneath its cliffs only during exceptional years. In Scotland's present climate, the Ben falls a hair's breadth short of having a glacier.

Yet sadly, the popular impression of Ben Nevis is only the great hunched back with which it guards its treasures. The picture-postcard views from around Corpach are unflattering to say the least, and the besieged 'tourist track' to the summit – up whose tedious zigzags in summer thousands struggle wearing everything from wellies to high heels – reveals little of the mountain or the great 2km line of north-east facing cliffs.

Here then are described two routes worthy of the mountain. The first, approaching Ben Nevis by the celebrated Càrn Mòr Dearg Arête, requires only a reasonable head for heights. The second ascends Ledge Route – a devious and unlikely line through some of the mountain's most impressive cliff scenery which calls for confident scrambling – and tackles the Càrn Mòr Dearg Arête in the opposite direction.

Both itineraries begin at the golf course south of Inverlochy Castle, gaining the mountain by the narrowing glen of the Allt a' Mhuilinn. At the time of writing the golf club car park is closed to non-members, but there is a parking lay-by on the A82 300m west of the club, and room along the verge should this be full. Please park considerately.

From the club car park, a track leads under the West Highland Railway line, soon spawning a path which crosses the golf course to a morass below a gate in a fence bordering the scrubby woods of the lower Allt a' Mhuilinn. The path is obvious, braiding muddily through the trees, and climbing beside a fence to more open and level ground. Beyond a dam and rusting crane, a track emerging from the densely planted conifers of the Leanachan Forest is followed to a car park where authorised outdoor centres and guides often leave vehicles.

A stile crosses a deer fence to a notoriously boggy section of moorland, whose first 1.5km has been improved immeasurably by

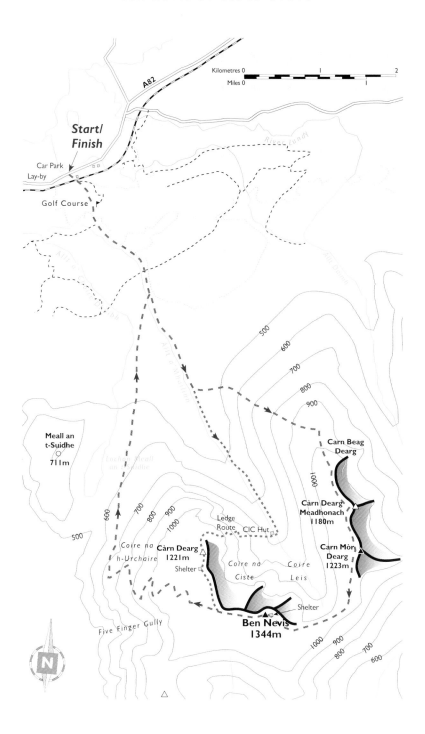

path repairs. By now the cliffs of the Ben are starting to loom. The two routes described largely overlap – but in opposite directions, so it seems best to describe them separately. If choosing the less serious option, 1km or so after the stile bear off left up the featureless heathery north-west slopes of Càrn Beag Dearg until, at 1000m, a well-defined ridge is reached. This ascent is something of a grind, but provides rapid access to the high ground where things quickly improve. On clear days the views from onwards of the stony Top of Càrn Dearg Meadhonach have few British rivals.

The 1223m (4012ft) Càrn Mòr Dearg is next: a very fine summit, and the seventh highest Munro. Being here early in the day means that any sunlight will be bathing the great buttresses and gullies of the Ben opposite. Pre-eminent are the soaring wedge of the North East Buttress – all 500m of it; the wrinkled pillar of Observatory Ridge between Zero and Point Five gullies – possibly the most famous winter gully climbs in the world; the snaking barrier of Tower Ridge; and the impending rock mass of Càrn Dearg Buttress, atop which Ledge Route winds its improbable way. Southwards is an extraordinary panorama over the entire Mamore range to the peaks of Glen Coe and the southern Highlands.

Below, the Càrn Mòr Dearg Arête swoops gracefully around the barren head of Coire Leis to merge with the steep bouldery south-east slopes of Ben Nevis. Keen rock-hoppers should stick to the crest of very pink granite boulders, while those shy of such exuberance should keep left when in doubt. At one point the deliciously scrambly arête

The Càrn Mòr Dearg Arête from Càrn Mòr Dearg; Mamores behind.

mimics the crest of a stone wall, dropping vertically rightwards and to the left steeply for 900m into Glen Nevis, where the waterfall of An Steall rumbles off the side of An Gearanach in a fan of silver.

Abseil posts descending into Coire Leis (for emergency winter use) signal the end of the scrambling and a steep, rocky 210m grind to the summit of Ben Nevis, now on greyish andesite. The geology of Ben Nevis is fascinating. The mountain is a 'plug' of pale andesitic (a term descriptive of mineral composition) lavas and other volcanic deposits overlying metamorphic rocks (rocks altered usually as a result of pressure or heat), which collapsed into a vast subterranean bubble of molten rock known as a 'pluton' in a process called cauldron subsidence. The overlying rocks have worn away, exposing this like the yolk in a poached egg-white of plutonic granites.

The desolate flatness of the stony summit plateau, strewn with litter, cairns and other landmarks including the ruins of a Victorian observatory and an emergency shelter on a stone plinth (to prevent

No. 5 Gully and Càrn Dearg Buttress from the CIC Hut, Ben Nevis.

burial by snow), is a heady contrast to the Càrn Mòr Dearg Arête. W. T. Kilgour's record of life manning the observatory – which operated for 20 years from October 1883 – makes fascinating reading. It was serviced by a specially built pony track: now the 'tourist track'. Several proposals were made after the turn of the century for a railway up the narrow corridor of feasible ground used by the pony track. Although these mercifully fell through, the idea has recently been revived.

If time and conditions allow, a brief detour along the summit prow of the north-east Buttress gives vertiginous views of the cliffs and surrounding peaks. Even Càrn Mòr Dearg seems small from here. The view of the Mamores from Ben Nevis is like that from a plane. On a crystal day it really is possible to see all of the Highlands, and even across the distant lowlands to the Southern Uplands.

The descending path angles around the head of Gardyloo Gully, with views of Tower Ridge and its notorious 'gap'. Gardyloo Gully was the Observatory's sewer, named after the Edinburgh cry of 'gardyloo!' (from the French *Gardez-l'eau*), made when chamber pots were emptied from windows into street gutters below. In winter and spring, huge cornices can make it a dangerous place. In poor visibility with snow obscuring the path, this and the notorious Five Finger Gully – which has claimed many lives – can be avoided by following a grid bearing of 231º for 150m from the summit trig point, then 281º until clear of the plateau. Controversial marker posts were installed in summer 1996 to aid navigation in emergencies, but may have been removed by the time this book is published.

In summer though the path is usually all too obvious, descending in huge zigzags towards the desolate Lochan Meall an t-Suidhe at a height of 565m. On the first Saturday in September, in the annual Ben Nevis Race, fell-runners hare up to the summit and back. The record time is less than 90 minutes up and down. Adding insult to injury, wheel-barrows, beds, pianos, motorcycles, and even a car have found their way up here.

A path branches northwards from the track into Glen Nevis, cutting over the shoulder of Càrn Dearg and traversing into the glen of the Allt a' Mhuilinn towards the Charles Inglis Clark (CIC) Hut (privately owned by the Scottish Mountaineering Club, and a mountaineering legend). For those with energy left, this detour provides superb perspectives of the cliffs – but otherwise, from above the lochan just follow heathery slopes north, cross the Allt a' Mhuilinn above the deer fence, and descend to the golf course.

If opting for Ledge Route, follow the path up the Allt a' Mhuilinn as far as the CIC Hut. Above, Càrn Dearg Buttress hangs with damoclean intent: a most unlikely proposition. Nevertheless, climb from the hut towards the foot of the buttress, latterly up easy slabs, and follow the cliff-base leftwards into the jaws of No 5 Gully. In early summer there is usually snow here (ice-axe recommended: can be hired in Fort William), which is often soft enough to kick steps up. Alternatively, it can often be avoided by a slabby scramble to the right (harder than Ledge Route itself).

Around 60 metres up, a large terrace can be seen cutting back across the right wall of the gully. This is followed easily to a little rock step, beyond which – much narrower – it continues. Approximately 10m onwards, a sloping ramp rises leftwards through a line of weakness. It is quite vegetated and often wet, but not difficult, and should be followed to a viewpoint high above No 5 Gully, which gives superb perspectives of the Ben's enormous cliffs. Rightwards again, another sloping stony ramp gives straightforward walking past an obvious square-topped pinnacle to a shoulder marked by a perched boulder.

Here the real fun starts. The route follows the very crest of the Càrn Dearg Buttress: a narrow, twisting arête in a situation worthy of the Cuillin of Skye. Soon, alas, the ridge bifurcates into blunter ribs, from which easier ground leads to a final steepening and the sudden flatness of 1221m (3961ft) Càrn Dearg's summit plateau.

From here, stride south to the dip between Càrn Dearg and the rest of Ben Nevis, picking up the pony track and following it to the summit. Descending now over Càrn Mòr Dearg and its arête provides one of the finest expeditions the Ben has to offer.

WALK 2

THE AONACHS
AND THE GREY CORRIES

Distance: 21.5km (13.5 miles).
Ascent: 1710m (5610ft).
Start: Nevis Range Ski car park (GR171773), signposted from A82 8km (5 miles) north of Fort William.
Finish: Corriechoille (GR250807).
Maps: OS Landranger 41 *Ben Nevis, Fort William & surrounding area* or Outdoor Leisure 38 *Ben Nevis & Glencoe* or Pathfinders 277 *Ben Nevis & Fort William*, 278 *Loch Treig* and 265 *Spean Bridge & Glen Roy*. Harveys Walker's Map or Superwalker *Glen Coe*.
Terrain: The figures may be misleading: this is a demanding outing. Aonach Mòr and Aonach Beag provide easy walking over broad whalebacks, but require diligent navigation in poor visibility, especially on Aonach Mòr. The rest of the walk is a rollercoaster of rough and often quite narrow ridges. Care is needed locating the easiest way down the steep eastern escarpment of Stob Coire Bhealaich.
Stalking information: Mamores and Grey Corries Hillphone Service, tel. 01855 831511 (August-late October).

Gaelic names

   Aonach Mor/Beag (oe:noch **moa:r/bayk**): Big/little ridge.
   Coire an Lochain (kora an **loch**Yn`): Corrie of the lochan.
   Stob Coire Bhealaich (stob kora **vya**leech): Peak of the corrie of the pass.
   Meall Cumhann (myowl **coo**-an): Given the mountain's commanding position above the Nevis Gorge, probably from *meall cumhang* (**coo**-ang), meaning mound of the defile.
   Sgurr a' Bhuic (skoor a **voo**eechk): Peak of the buck.

Top: The Grey Corries from above Spean Bridge.

Sgùrr Chòinnich Beag/Mòr (skoor chawnyeech **bayk/moa:r**): Little/Big peak of the moss.

Stob Coire Easain (stob kora **es**Yn): Peak of the corrie of the little waterfalls.

Stob Coire an Laoigh (stob kora an **loe**-ee): Peak of the corrie of the calf.

Caisteal (**kash**tyal): Castle.

Stob Coire Cath na Sine (stob kora **ca** na **shee**na): Peak of the corrie of the battle of the elements.

Stob a' Choire Lèith (stob a chora **lyay**): Peak of the grey corrie.

Stob Choire Claurigh (stop chora **klow**ree): Possibly peak of the corrie of clamouring (from the Gaelic *clamhras*).

Stob Coire Gaibhre (stob kora **gY**ra): Peak of the corrie of the goat.

Beinn Bhàn (bYn **vaan**): Pale mountain.

Stob Coire na Ceannain (stob kora na **kyown**Yn): Peak of the corrie of the little head.

Làirig Leacach (la:reek **lyech**koch): Slabby pass or pass of the flat rock (possibly pass of the bare mountain top).

Known collectively as 'The Aonachs', Aonach Mòr and Aonach Beag – eighth and sixth highest Munros at 1219m (3999ft) and 1236m (4060ft) respectively – form the start of this challenging walk. Though lacking the authority of their neighbour Ben Nevis they are massive, steep-sided mountains, forming an east-facing escarpment of cliffs 6km in length. On Aonach Beag this precipice reaches spectacular dimensions, the corrie beneath being one of the most impressive in the Highlands, with a floor 800m (2630ft) below the top of the beetling crags.

Named for their silvery screes, the neighbouring 'Grey Corries' are a fine group of four Munros and eight Tops, providing glorious walking along a stark spine of shattered quartzite which only once falls below 914m (3000ft), and stunning views of the Aonachs and Ben Nevis. When combined with the Aonachs their traverse is one of the finest outings in the Central Highlands.

This walk is best enjoyed if two vehicles are available, one of which can be left near the farm of Corriechoille. Parking opportunities exist before the farm – or alternatively, driving up the unsurfaced private road to the south is currently tolerated as far as a grassy parking area below the forestry plantation. Another option is to leave a bicycle here for the return to the Nevis Range ski car park, where the day begins.

Established in 1990 as a western rival to the skiing centres at Cairngorm and Glenshee, the Nevis Range ski developments have had a considerable visual impact on Aonach Mòr. The bottom station with its huge bare car park amidst regiments of planted

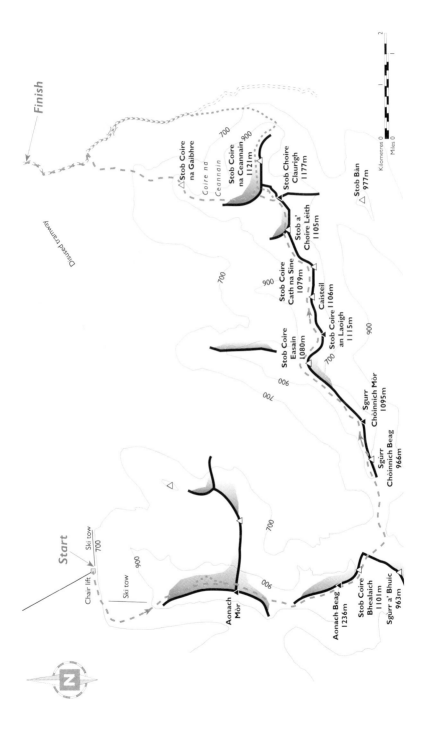

Finish

Disused tramway

Start

Chair lift

Ski tow

Ski tow

Ski tow

900

700

Aonach Mór 1236m

Aonach Beag 1101m

Stob Coire Bhealaich 1101m

Sgùrr a' Bhuic 963m

Sgùrr Chòinnich Beag 966m

Sgùrr Chòinnich Mór 1095m

Stob Coire an Laoigh 1115m

Caisteil 1106m

Stob Coire Easain 1080m

Stob Coire Cath na Sine 1079m

Stob a' Choire Léith 1105m

Stob Choire Claurigh 1177m

Stob Coire na Ceannain 1121m

Stob Coire na Gaibhre

Coire na Ceannain

Stob Bàn 977m

700

900

700

900

700

900

700

900

900

Kilometres 0 1 2

Miles 0 1

Sgurr a' Bhuic and Stob Coire Bhealaich from upper Glen Nevis.

conifers, is a starkly functional place, and the top station at 655m resembles a brightly painted warehouse. The gondola allows an effortless start to the day and a quicker escape to unspoiled scenery, but there is a path climbing more or less below the pylons for any who regard such mechanised uplift as cheating.

From the top station a track leads west to a ski-tow. Just beyond, slant up the mountain's bowl-shaped northern slope towards its western edge, which is followed up onto Aonach Mòr's summit plateau. The ground grows increasingly rocky, with precipices to the right and views of graceful ridges falling eastwards from Càrn Mòr Dearg. The ski-tows may be an intrusion, but a summer ascent will at least avoid the din of their engines, which sometimes carries to neighbouring peaks.

Having gained the impressively bleak and lengthy plateau, it is worth following its eastern edge briefly to appreciate the cliff-fringed bowl of Coire an Lochain. Gargantuan cornices form here, often persisting well into summer. In winter the plateau is a serious place, and even during the warmer months a close eye should be kept on map and compass. The summit cairn is marooned amidst the moss and stones; the best views being obtained about 100m south-west, from where Ben Nevis looms over the simple elegance of Càrn Mòr Dearg.

A gentle descent to a quite narrow neck separating the two Aonachs precedes an initially steep 140m rise to the great bald summit dome of Aonach Beag. There is truth in the mountains' apparently topsy-turvy Gaelic names: although lower, as a ridge Aonach Mòr is now clearly much bigger than Aonach Beag. Aonach Mòr lies within the

Stob Bàn and Stob Choire Claurigh from Sgùrr Innse.

granite encircling Ben Nevis, but Aonach Beag is mainly schist: the highest British peak of metamorphic rock. It also sports outcrops of the highest limestone.

The cairn of its lofty wild summit neighbours the edge of the great eastern cliffs – another site for monstrous cornices. From up here the Grey Corries look deceptively gentle, but from west of the cairn you get extremely impressive views of Ben Nevis plunging from its half-dome summit to the floor of Glen Nevis fully 1240m below. The 698m peak of Meall Cumhann, so impressive from Glen Nevis, seems barely a hummock.

Follow the descending rim of the cliffs SSE. A path skirts the rocky 1101m Top of Stob Coire Bhealaich (which can be pleasantly traversed) before progress is barred by a continuation of Aonach Beag's eastern face which kinks SSW as far as the mountain's pointed quartzite satellite, Sgùrr a' Bhuic. Descend above this escarpment to a small dip on its crest (GR206705), 200m before its low point below Sgùrr a' Bhuic and just south of a prominent prow-shaped buttress. Here, a generally straightforward grassy gully descends eastwards until a rough traverse can be made onto the broad, knolly bealach below the first peak of the Grey Corries: Sgùrr Chòinnich Beag.

The pull up to this 966 Top is a steady 230m, and the climb to big Munro sister Sgùrr Chòinnich Mòr is similar, but wilder. Its 1095m (3603ft) summit, which earlier looked so small, feels like the top of the world, and is a fine place from which to appreciate Aonach Beag. Now level with them, the Mamores across the bleak upper reaches of Glen Nevis also look splendid – especially chisel-topped Binnein

Mòr looming over the remarkably conical Binnein Beag. There is also a surprisingly good view of the distant Buachaille Etive Mòr.

The descent which follows is a delight: dipping ridges and levellings until steeper ground leads to a bealach adjoining the quartzite prow of the next Top, Stob Coire Easain. An interesting feature here is a pavement of silvery-white quartzite, split by fissures that will swallow a person. There follows a steep and very rough rise to Stob Coire Easain's cairn at 1080m (3545ft): a fine vantage point for the headwaters of the beautiful River Cour rising in Aonach Beag's huge eastern corrie.

The ensuing ridge is an exhilarating switchback. It turns ESE to the 1115m (3657ft) Munro of Stob Coire an Laoigh, dog-legs north-east over the Top of Caisteal, kinks east over another Top, Stob Coire Cath na Sine, north-east again over the slightly better defined Top of Stob a' Choire Lèith – all on the same eerily skeletal layered quartzite – and finally curves east again, climbing to the highest of the Grey Corries and the day's final Munro: 1177m (3858ft) Stob Choire Claurigh. The ridge is never scrambly or narrow enough to present difficulties; yet the walking, and the views, back over a succession of ever higher peaks, are of such quality that there is never a dull moment.

From Stob Choire Claurigh the most straightforward descent is north via the shy 955m (3134ft) Top of Stob Coire Gaibhre and the easy north slopes of Beinn Bhan; following the plantation fence down to the track descending from the Làirig Leacach. An easy final scramble can be enjoyed however by making a 500m detour from Stob Coire Gaibhre along the blocky arête which dips east to the finely pointed 1121m (3679ft) Top of Stob Coire na Ceannain, high above the almost circular lochan adorning the corrie from which the peak takes its name.

The most knee-friendly descent from here is via a return to Stob Coire Gaibhre. Those to whom aesthetic purity is important, however, could descend eastwards, slanting north before the eastern ridge steepens into crags for a slightly lengthier march down the Làirig Leacach track to Corriechoille.

WALK 3

SGÙRR INNSE
AND CRUACH INNSE

Distance: 17km (10.5 miles).
Ascent: 1000m (3280ft).
Start/Finish: Turn off A82 just west of the junction with A86 at Spean Bridge and follow a minor road for 3.5km, continuing along a private road past Corriechoille farm. 2km along this road, there is a parking space just before the plantation (GR256788).
Maps: OS Landranger 41 *Ben Nevis, Fort William & surrounding area* or Pathfinders 265 *Spean Bridge and Glen Roy* and 278 *Loch Treig.*
Terrain: Good unsurfaced track (bicycle a great asset) followed by generally straightforward though sometimes steep walking; mostly on grassy heath. Some slightly trickier ground, especially on Sgùrr Innse, though scrambling is never necessary.
Stalking information: Mamores and Grey Corries Hillphone Service, tel. 01855 831511 (August-late October).

Gaelic names

Sgurr Innse (skoor **ee:n**sha): Island peak
Cruach Innse (croo-ach **ee:n**sha): Island heap
Allt Leachdach (owlt **lyech**doch): Stream of the slab or flat rock.
Lairig Leacach (la:reek **lyech**koch): Slabby pass or pass of the flat rock (possibly pass of the bare mountain top).
Stob Coire na Ceannain (stob kora na **kyown**Yn'): Peak of the corrie of the little head.
Stob Coire Easain (stob Kora **es**Yn): Peak of the corrie of little water falls.
Stob a'Coire Mheadhoin (stob a chora **vee**-oin): Peak of the middle corrie.

Top: Stob Bàn and Sgùrr Ìnnse from above Loch Laggan.

These two Corbetts provide an interesting and fairly relaxed day out, and are far more likely to offer solitude than the surrounding Munros. An off-road bicycle will add greatly to the experience, as the first 3km are on a sometimes rough unsurfaced track. This follows part of the ancient cattle droving route known as the 'Road to the Isles', down which cattlemen from as far away as the island of Skye used to drive their herds to sell them at the trysts in Falkirk and Crieff – an arduous journey of more than 260km, made even more remarkable by the fact that their dogs would return home unaccompanied! The Làirig Leacach, above which Sgurr Innse and the conical Munro of Stob Bàn stand opposed like sentinels, was one of the key passes on this route.

From Spean Bridge a narrow road winds through glorious woods above the gorge of the River Spean until a signpost indicates the right of way over the Làirig Leacach to Rannoch. Past the farm of Corriechoille, a rough private road leads to a parking space.

Fringing the plantation is a dismantled railway, whose sleepers now line the road. This was used during the construction of a tunnel supplying the British Aluminium Company's factory at Fort William with water from Loch Treig. A stile and gate lead to a broad track through the trees – sufficiently steep to make pedalling hard work, but a bike will be appreciated later, and the shade is deliciously cool on a hot day. Another gate marks the far side of the conifers. The track follows the plantation's edge for 200m before levelling and dropping to an outsize modern bridge over the lively Allt Leachdach, which is also scarred by a recent ford.

Cruach Innse looms above the scene like a large steamed pudding, providing an opportunity to note a small crag on its convex

Sgùrr Innse from the Làirig Leacach.

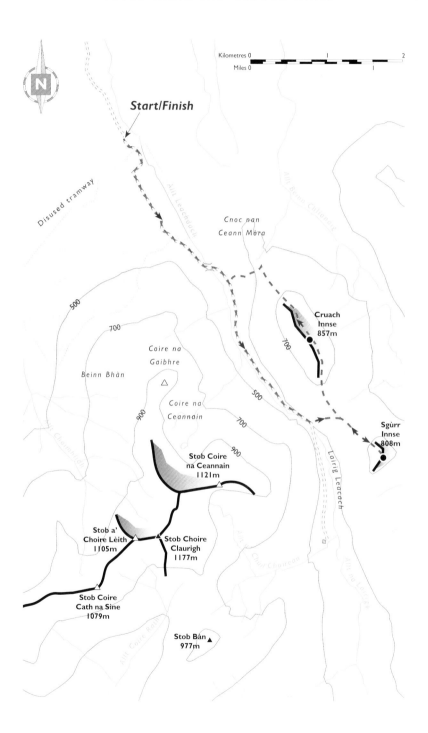

Start/Finish

Kilometres 0   1   2

Miles 0   1

Disused tramway

500

700

Cnoc nan
Ceann Mòra

Coire na
Gaibhre

Beinn Bhàn

Coire na
Ceannain

900

700

500

Cruach
Innse
857m

700

Sgùrr
Innse
808m

Lairig Leacach

Stob Coire
na Ceannain
1121m

900

Stob a'
Choire Lèith
1105m

Stob Choire
Claurigh
1177m

Stob Coire
Cath na Sine
1079m

Stob Bàn
977m

northern slopes to avoid later on. The track mounts the Cruach's flank before turning towards the Làirig Leacach. Cyclists planning the circular walk described could leave their bikes where the track crosses a small burn (not shown on the 1:50 000 map) trickling down from north of Cruach Innse, which is a useful guide for the descent.

The track now provides a pleasant tramp of around 2km through ever improving scenery, with the birch-scattered banks of the Allt Leachdach below and the rocky pyramid of Stob Coire na Ceannain high above. Further towards the Làirig the slopes of the Cruach grow rougher, with a huge block perched alarmingly on the skyline. Sgùrr Innse comes into view – like a craggy jelly in contrast to its quite pointed appearance from the south.

A little beyond a ford in the burn is the best place to leave the track. Cross the peat-hagged floor of the summit of the Làirig, and angle rightwards up slopes of grassy heath to gain the bealach between Cruach Innse and Sgùrr Innse. Helpfully, the Làirig is at an altitude of 495m - which leaves just 90m of climbing to the bealach and only 313m to the summit of Sgùrr Innse! Pick a way up the Sgùrr's broad lower ridge between knolls of pinkish quartzite, from where Cruach Innse is still suspiciously pudding-like. The assertive little peak of Stob Bàn emerges above a lonely bothy and stable in the flats to the south.

In cropped heath at the foot of two obvious rock fans is an artistically arranged group of angular boulders, fallen from the triangular cliff above. A vegetated ramp between the fans – which between August and September overflows with delicious fat purple blaeberries (*Vaccinium myrtillus*) – develops a tiny path which trends leftwards below steep broken ground, crossing the top of the left-hand fan and then fading. Head uphill for 20-30m then continue rising leftwards along an obvious break in the broken ground, where the path grows clearer again, eventually bearing rightwards before a hollow on the peak's north side.

A series of rocky steps – which can be avoided by traversing rightwards along a grassy terrace until a clear path loops back up to the left – lead to the 808m (2651ft) summit. This is a bit of a surprise; its tiny cairn crowns a choppy plateau of a couple of acres. Horizons are limited by higher surrounding peaks, but Stob Choire Claurigh to the west and the twin Easains (Stob Coire Easain and Stob a' Choire Mheadhoin) to the south-east look fine. Southwards are the Crianlarich hills, Ben Lui, the Blackmount summits and the peaks of Glen Coe, but not from their best angle. The glens immediately north and west are eerily stark and bare.

The return to the bealach is by the same route. A broad hummocky ridge rambles to the foot of Cruach Innse; a sketchy path climbs steeply between the rocks of the first rise, which at the top is wet and

The Easains from Sgùrr Innse.

dotted with bog-cotton (*Eriophorum vaginatum*). From here pick a left-trending line up through more blaeberries until the ridge above is reached and a faint path picked up. This shortly traverses left around craggy ground before rising steeply to the ridge again.

Another outcrop is soon bypassed by the now obvious path, which negotiates some delightfully intricate schistose rock scenery: much more fun than was evident from Sgùrr Innse. Gradually the ridge broadens and levels into a great whaleback, vegetated nutrient-rich schist changing abruptly to barren whitish quartzite clung with rags of wind-stripped vegetation, leading to a squat cairn capping the domed 857m (2812ft) summit.

Sgùrr Innse looks very timid from here, utterly dwarfed by the Easains. Although the Sgùrr was a generally better viewpoint, Cruach Innse adds perspectives of the rolling eastern Central Highlands: the hills of the Ardverikie and Ben Alder Forests, Creag Meagaidh above Loch Laggan, northwards over the broad open Strath of the River Spean, and west past Loch Eil towards distant Moidart and Knoydart.

The descent to the track via the steepening grassy ridge to the north doesn't take very long, and the return cycle will take but minutes. The speeds possible on the forest track can easily induce gibbering long before the forest exit gate, but beware of invisible bumps, pedestrians, and some nasty blind corners. Above all, wear a helmet and make sure your brakes are good!

WALK 4

THE WESTERN MAMORES

Distance: 20km (12.5 miles).
Ascent: 2200m (7220ft).
Start/finish: Glen Nevis roadhead car park (GR167692).
Maps: OS Landranger 41 *Ben Nevis, Fort William & surrounding area* or Outdoor Leisure 38 *Ben Nevis & Glencoe* or Pathfinder 290 *Kinlochleven.* Harveys Walker's Map or Superwalker *Glen Coe.*
Terrain: Spectacular walking through the Nevis gorge, followed by a steep initial ascent and superb high-level ridge walking with easy but often exposed sections of scrambling. On one section, the 'Devil's Ridge', less confident scramblers might appreciate a rope.
Stalking Information: Mamores and Grey Corries Hillphone Service, tel. 01855 831511 (August-late October).

Gaelic names

Mamores: probably from màm mòr (maam **moa:r**), meaning big breast (referring to hill shapes).
Allt Coire Eògbain: mis-spelling of *allt coire Eòbhainn* (owlt Kora **Yaw**Yn^y): Stream of Ewan's corrie.
An Steall (an **shtyowl**): The spout.
An Gearanach (an **gya**ranoch): The complainer.
An Garbhanach (an **ga**ravanoch): The rough one.
Stob Coire a' Chairn (stob kor a **chaarn**): Peak of the corrie of the cairn.
Am Bodach (am **bo**toch): The old man.
Sgurr an Iubhair (skor an **yoo**ar): Peak of the yew.
Stob a' Choire mhail (stob a kora **vaal**): Possibly from stob a' choire màl: peak of the corrie of the rent.
Sgùrr à Mhàim (skoor a **vaa**-eem): Peak of the breast.
Lochan Coire nam Mìseach (lochan kora nam **mee**shoch): Lochan of the corrie of the kids.
Stob Ban (stob **baan**): Pale hill.

Top: The wire bridge in Glen Nevis.
Opposite: An Steall.

Mullach nan Coirean (mooloch nan **kor**yan): Top of the corries.

Coire Dearg (Kora **dye**rak): red corrie.

Allt a'Choire Dhèirg (owlt a chore **ye**rak): stream of the red corrie.

The Mamores have been described as one of the finest mountain ranges in Britain – and with some justification, for while largely lacking the bold features of the great individual peaks, they compensate by collectively offering scenery and walking of a quality and variety to be found in few other places. Access into the range is eased enormously by a fine network of stalkers' paths; originally constructed under often terrible conditions by workers of the great deer estates to enable easier removal of kills from the high tops by deer stalkers and their ponies.

The traverse of all eleven Munros and six Tops of the Mamores is a magnificent expedition, but as well as being a little demanding for the scope of this book, it is probably best to savour the range at a more relaxed pace. The two walks described cover most of the group's finest features.

Covering the western half of the Mamores, the first walk begins in Glen Nevis: a glen with few equals. The scenery here is on a scale nearly half as large again as any British counterpart, with 914m (3000ft) peaks on all sides dominated by the overpowering bulk of Ben Nevis, rising 1300m from a glen floor virtually at sea-level. Swathes of mixed woodland still survive on their flanks, and above Polldubh the glen's sole concession to development is a single track road and car-park at its head.

The Allt Coire Eògbain forms a continuous waterslide for 460m down the flank of Ben Nevis – the longest in Britain. From the often overcrowded car park near its base, an excellent wide path heads off into lush woodlands beneath the imposing craggy peak of Meall Cumhann, above which, twice as high, looms Aonach Beag. Willow, hazel, rowan, birch, Scots pine and wild roses ensure that autumn colours here are spectacular – as is the path. Sometimes carved from the rock, it curves high above the torrent of the Water of Nevis, giving glorious views down the glen.

The path enters a narrow defile carved by enormous volumes of meltwater from the glaciers which once occupied the glen and its tributaries, where the river squeezes between huge boulders and water-smoothed cliffs. With dramatic suddenness, the scene changes completely, the path dropping into a gentle vale of cropped meadows, behind which a 110m waterfall – An Steall – tumbles between two forested buttresses of silvery quartzite below the Munro of An Gearanach.

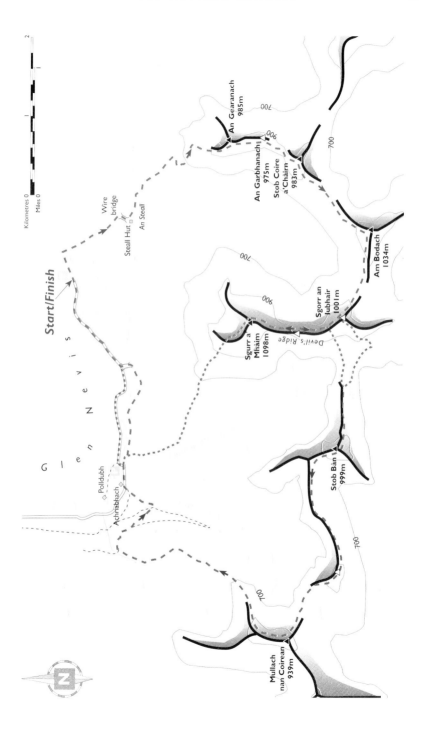

Kilometres 0
Miles 0

Start/Finish

Glen Nevis

Wire bridge

Steall Hut

An Steall

Polldubh

Achriabhach

An Gearanach 985m

An Garbhanach 975m

Stob Coire a'Chàirn 983m

Am Bodach 1034m

Sgorr an Iubhair 1001m

Sgurr a' Mhàim 1098m

Devil's Ridge

Stob Bàn 999m

Mullach nan Coirean 939m

700

900

700

700

900

900

700

700

Had they materialised, plans to dam the glen in the 1940s would have made the world a poorer place. It is hard to believe that the industrial sprawl of Fort William is just around the corner, although the meadows can be busy. Follow the well-worn path through the meadows for 500m until the glen kinks leftwards, then bear towards a bridge of three wobbling wires tensioned across the Water of Nevis at a deep pool: the first excitement of the day. On the far side a path skirts the beautifully situated Steall Hut (run by the Lochaber Mountaineering Club), continuing boggily below dense birchwoods towards An Steall.

It is thoroughly worth a brief detour to the foot of the falls, but the Allt Coire a' Mhail is most easily crossed 200m downstream. Beyond, a path climbs a grassed-over debris fan, crossing another stream before climbing the terminal moraines of the glacier which died not so long ago in the little north corrie of An Gearanach. It

An Garbhanach and an Gearanach, Stob a' Choire Mhail and Sgùrr a' Mhàim from Upper Glen Nevis.

crosses the stream again, then makes innumerable zigzags up the corrie headwall before breaking rightwards below the crags onto the mountain's north-east arm. This is climbed without difficulty, giving increasingly wild views of the glen and the hunched muscular shoulders of Ben Nevis, to the summit at 985m (3230ft).

The ridge running south is an airy walk, narrowing into a fine arête on the climb to the 975m (3206ft) Top of An Garbhanach, with an exposed and very narrow rocky step. The descent southwards is quite steep and scrambly, but also short; leaving an equally brief climb to the unremarkable 983m (3219ft) Munro of Stob Coire a' Chairn.

From here a pleasant grassy walkway leads south-west to the rocky north-east ridge of Am Bodach: a fairly brutal ascent to a fine summit at 1032m (3382ft). More easy grass leads onwards to the flat, stony summit of Sgòrr an Iubhair, from where the quartzite half-cone of Stob Bàn looks quite magnificent. The 2.5km detour which follows is the best bit of the route, rivalled only by An Garbhanach. It includes the Devil's Ridge: exposed easy scrambling north of the Top of Stob a' Choire Mhail, on which some may welcome the security of a rope. From Stob a' Choire Mhail a narrow crest dips over a couple of awkward rocky sections before a stiff 195m pull up to the cairn of Sgurr a' Mhaim – which, at 1099m (3601ft), proves every bit as good a viewpoint as promised.

Anyone who has had enough could now descend the mountain's north-west ridge all the way to the car park at Polldubh. Otherwise repeat the Devil's Ridge, which is probably even better in the opposite direction. Between Stob a' Choire Mhail and Sgòrr an Iubhair, two options present themselves: a steep drop west to Lochan Coire nam Mìseach, or a traverse above the western crags of Sgòrr an Iubhair before descending its bouldery western slopes. The lochan option gives perhaps more variety, but is steep: both alternatives lead westwards to a broad bealach below Stob Bàn – at around 760m, the lowest on the walk. A stiff ascent around Stob Bàn's impressive quartzite crags leads to a fine 999m (3274ft) summit.

An arm thrusts northwards to a minor Top, from where a ridge falls westwards before climbing gradually towards the south-east Top of Mullach nan Coirean. From here, look back at the Mullach's bright red granite against the silver-white quartzite of Stob Bàn: a quite startling clash of colours. Although the aptly named 939m (3077ft) Mullach nan Coirean is the most lumpen of the Mamores, its lazy plateau is the perfect way to finish a satisfying day, with Loch Linnhe to the west and a panoply of surrounding hills. Linger a while at the summit cairn, then skirt the broken crags of Coire Dearg, descending the broadening ridge to the east.

On the arête between An Gearanach and An Garbhanach.

A path is picked up descending to a deer fence, which is followed down as far as the Allt a' Choire Dhèirg – the westernmost of two neighbouring streams of that name. Here cross the fence: a path shadows the stream through scrubby birchwoods down to recently clear-felled plantations and a forestry road slanting down across the hillside. Where this doubles back on itself a waymarked path descends to the Glen Nevis road, which leads directly back to the walk's starting point. Alternatively, a path on the opposite side of the glen can be followed for 1.5km as far as a bridge across the Water of Nevis.

WALK 5

THE EASTERN MAMORES

Distance: 20km (12.5km).
Ascent: 1630m (5340ft).
Start/finish: Mamore Lodge (GR186630), reached by turning off B863 just over 1km west of Kinlochleven.
Maps: OS Landranger 41 *Ben Nevis, Fort William & surrounding* area or Outdoor Leisure 38 *Ben Nevis & Glencoe* or Pathfinders 290 *Kinlochleven* and 291 *Mamore Forest*. Harveys Walker's Map and Superwalker *Ben Nevis*.
Terrain: High-level ridge walking, with some steep and mildly scrambly sections, with optional scrambling on Binnein Mòr. The initial ascent and final descent are eased enormously by stalkers' paths.
Stalking information: Mamores and Grey Corries Hillphone Service, tel. 01855 831511 (August-late October).

Gaelic names
    Allt Coire na Bà (owlt kora na **baa**): Stream of the corrie of cattle.
    Sgòr Eilde Beag (skor ay:ltya **bayk**): Little peak of the hind.
    Sgùrr Eilde Mòr (skoor ay:ltya **moa:r**): Big peak of the hind.
    Coire an Lochain (kora an **loch**Yn): Corrie of the lochan.
    Coire a' Bhinnein (kora a **veen**yan): Corrie of the peak.
    Allt Coire a' Bhinnein (owlt kora a **veen**yan): Stream of the corrie of the peak.
    Binnein Beag (beenyan **bayk**): Little peak.
    Binnein Mòr (beenyan **moa:r**): Big peak.
    Abhainn Rath (avYn **raa**): Origin obscure (abhainn means river).
    Na Gruagaichean (na **groo**ageechan): The maidens.

This walk takes in all the remaining Mamores, with the exception of Sgùrr Eilde Mòr – a fine peak and viewpoint, but not easy to fit into a logical two-day itinerary. The best starting point is Mamore Lodge, 200m above the tidal waters of

Top: The Glen Coe peaks and Kinlochleven from Na Gruagaichean.

Loch Leven, reached by a private track just over 1km west of Kinlochleven. Walkers can currently leave vehicles here for a small fee.

Alternatively, for those without personal transport, several paths approach the route from Kinlochleven, the most interesting of which visits the Grey Mare's Tail. Although neighbouring a less than lovely industrial town, this underrated 50m waterfall on the Allt Coire na Bà is very fine indeed. From the viewing platform, the waterfall's height and position mean that only part of the fall can be seen, but in spate its thundering gives an impressive sense of power, magnified by its confined woodland situation below the steep flanks of the Mamores. The woods hereabouts are well worth exploring on their own. A good time to visit is late spring, when their floor becomes a carpet of bluebells.

Once used as a shooting lodge by Edward VII, Mamore Lodge is an imposing and magnificently situated house, close to the old military road to Fort William, which is here followed by Scotland's best-known long-distance footpath, the West Highland Way. From the lodge, a track rises gradually eastwards through scrubby woodland at the foot of the Mamores, kinking northwards to cross the Allt Coire na Bà, before continuing around to lochs Eilde Mòr and Beag, and eventually descending 11.5km later to the remote bothy at Luibeilt.

About 3.5km along this track, an impressively constructed stalkers' path climbs up the hillside, giving excellent views – slightly marred by the ulceration of Kinlochleven – of the Pap of Glencoe and the gloriously wood-encrusted banks of Loch Leven. After some steady climbing it curves around the foot of Sgòr Eilde Beag, contouring above a crinkly lochan nestling on a broad bealach between Sgòr Eilde Beag and the (from here) very volcano-like Sgùrr Eilde Mòr.

The lochan between Binneins Mòr and Beag.

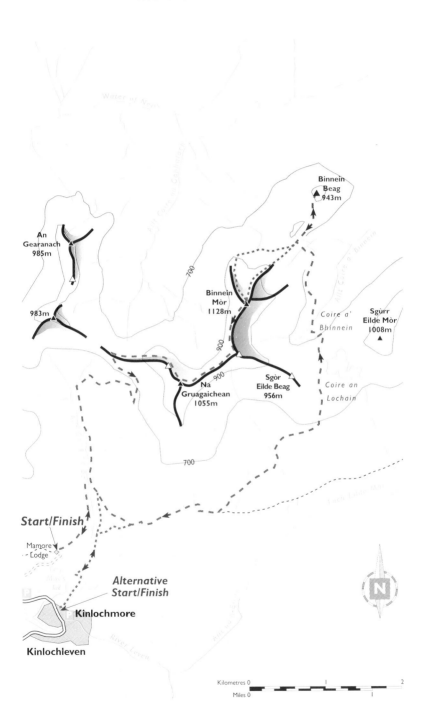

Binnein
Beag
943m

An
Gearanach
985m

983m

Binnein
Mòr
1128m

Sgùrr
Eilde Mòr
1008m

Coire a'
Bhinnein

700

900

Na
Gruagaichean
1055m

Sgòr
Eilde Beag
956m

900

Coire an
Lochain

700

Start/Finish

Mamore
Lodge

Alternative
Start/Finish

Kinlochmore

Kinlochleven

River Leven

Kilometres 0   1   2
Miles 0   1

Called Coire an Lochain, this is a beautiful, thoroughly wild spot - but things feel wilder still as the path descends northwards into Coire a' Bhinnein, which has a pronounced air of isolation. Having crossed the Allt Coire a' Bhinnein, the path makes a steadily rising traverse beneath the towering craggy walls of Binnein Mòr, eventually reaching another lochan, similarly situated but smaller; perched between the peaks of Binneins Beag and Mòr. Binnein Beag is an almost perfect cone from most angles, but from here a surprisingly well-defined ridge of bare quartzite gives a very enjoyable 210m clamber to the summit.

Though dwarfed by all of its neighbours, 940m (3083ft) Binnein Beag is a good viewpoint over the desolate headwaters of the Water of Nevis and and the Abhainn Rath. Binnein Mòr looks quite splendid from here, with its armchair-like eastern corrie. Having returned to the foot of Binnein Mòr, the rocky ridge defining this corrie's northern side provides some thoroughly enjoyable scrambling; but if wishing to avoid a moderate scramble, the best option is to cross the mountain's northern corrie and angle up onto its well defined NNW ridge.

From this corrie Binnein Mòr is needle-sharp, with a steep face of impressive parallel ribs of almost vertically dipping differentially eroded quartzite beds. The NNW ridge provides a straightforward ascent to a marvellously narrow and airy summit ridge. This superb 1128m (3700ft) peak is the highest and finest of the Mamores, and the views from its summit cairn are some of the best in this book.

From here a very pleasant ridge walk leads down over Binnein Mòr's 1059m (3476ft) south Top, from where a detour is possible to the mountain's other Top, Sgòr Eilde Beag. The dip to the foot of the splendidly named Na Gruagaichean (try saying that after a few drinks!) is not a long one, and neither is the following ascent to the higher of the mountain's twin summits at 1055m (3442ft).

The lower 1036m (3404ft) north-west Top looks very impressive from here, against the sharp horn of the Càrn Mòr Dearg Arête on the other side of Glen Nevis. The abrupt 60m (200ft) descent to the gap between the two peaks is rocky and very steep, and the equally steep ascent to the north-west Top impressively exposed on its north-east side above Coire an Easain. The excitement is over now: after a short, level summit promenade, an easy grassy ridge leads north-west down to a bealach, from which a stalker's path is followed into the corrie to the south.

This path does rather a lot of traversing and in places grows a little boggy and indistinct, but still provides a descent far easier (and less damaging to the vegetation) than the open hillside. In time it joins the track followed earlier, 1km from Mamore Lodge.

WALK 6

BEINN NA CAILLICH
AND MÀM NA GUALAINN

Distance: 11km (7 miles). 17.5 km (11 miles) including return to starting point.
Ascent: 830m (2720ft).
Start: car park on south side of B863 1km west of Kinlochleven (GR176623).
Finish: B863, 500m west of Callert House (GR096604).
Maps: OS Landranger 41 *Ben Nevis, Fort William & surrounding area* or Outdoor Leisure *38 Ben Nevis & Glencoe* or Pathfinder 290 *Kinlochleven*. Harveys Walker's Map or Superwalker *Ben Nevis*.
Terrain: A steep ascent eased by stalkers' paths, then easy and delightful walking over spacious grassy ridges. The approach crosses a wooden bridge which is in a state of disrepair. Unless able to leave a bicycle/second vehicle near Callert House, walking or hitch-hiking along a narrow but usually quiet road is required to return to the starting point.
Stalking Information: Mamores & Grey Corries Hillphone Service, tel. 01855 831511 (August-late October).

Gaelic names
  Beinn na Caillich (bYn na **kal**yeech): Mountain of the old woman.
  Màm na Gualainn (ma:m na **goo**-aleen): Breast-shaped hill of the shoulder.
  Kinlochmore: Head of the big loch.
  Allt Nathrach (owlt **na**roch): Adder-like stream.
  Garbh Bheinn (**gar**av vYn): Rough mountain.
  Aonach Eagach (oe:noch egoch): Notched ridge.

Top: Màm na Gualainn and Beinn na Caillich from Loch Leven.

Loch Leven is arguably one of the most beautiful of sea-lochs. The steepness of the northern slopes defining its slender upper arm lend it an excitingly fjord-like character. Though rising short of 800m, they do so from the loch's narrowest point – less than a hundred metres wide – to wild, windswept ridges in a horizontal distance of only 1.15km: an average angle of nearly 35 degrees.

These slopes are one side of a ridge with two clearly defined summits – Beinn na Caillich (764m, 2507ft) and Màm na Gualainn (796m, 2612ft). Although separated by almost 3km and both over 2500ft, an intervening dip of just 112m means that only Màm na Gualainn merits Corbett status, but – at least once the initial grunt is over – this, combined with delightful going on short turf, ensures carefree ridge-walking par excellence. Màm na Gualainn may suffer as a photographic subject in comparison to more extrovert neighbours such as the Pap of Glencoe and the Mamores, but the views and walking it provides concede nothing.

For those without personal transport the best starting point is the school in Kinlochleven, opposite which the West Highland Way is signposted leading off into the woods. Otherwise, vehicles can be left in a small car park on the loch side of the road 750m from the school, just before the signposted track to Mamore Lodge. A couple of hundred metres along the road from the car park, a little past the Mamore Lodge track, a gravelly path strikes up the wooded hillside immediately west of a small stream, winding through bracken and stands of birch, at one point detouring around a fallen tree, and in places often wet.

Beinn na Caillich and Garbh Bheinn above Loch Leven, from Màm na Gualainn.

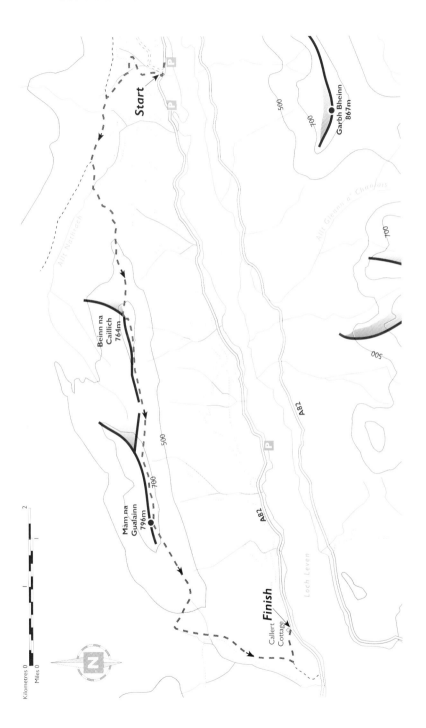

From Màm na Gualainn, looking across Loch Linnhe to Ardgour

Autumn is one of the best times to visit Loch Leven. Dank smells are brought to the nostrils crisp on chill air; the copper and gold of dying leaves just part of a heady kaleidoscope of colour: electric green and red mosses, outrageous orange swathes of bracken, rushes and grasses, and a clean-washed brittle blue sky. Having gained about 100m, the path joins the West Highland Way on its steady rise through the woods. The negative side of this footpath's enormous popularity is betrayed by litter and scarred banks; but this section, lovingly reconstructed in pitched stone, is still very beautiful indeed.

Before long the West Highland Way emerges from the trees, levelling off, then joining a wide track from Mamore Lodge, which heads west up the glen of the Allt Nathrach over a low pass before curving northwards down to Fort William. Beinn na Caillich looks steep from here, but the zigzags of the stalkers' path up it are

obvious. First, however, the descending path to the Allt Nathrach must be found – and given the blatancy of the path it leads to, this is surprisingly inconspicuous. The turn off is about 1km along the West Highland Way from its junction with the Mamore Lodge track, and the path is intermittent and muddy, becoming a rubble-floored slot lower down. The rotting bridge over the stream might give those phobic of river crossings an anxious moment or two.

The old deer estates certainly knew how to build their paths though, and the following ascent is easier than expected. Try comparing the effort you're expending with merely attacking a heathery slope. The path is eroding in places, and boggy in others, but leads with satisfying speed onto a broad heathery arm thrown down by Beinn na Caillich below its tent-shaped summit. The path peters out here but is regained again, traversing rightwards through blaeberries beneath the steep summit escarpment before crossing the mountain's shoulder above a lochan and angling up the north side of the ridge to an obvious gap. Of the cairn-topped grassy knolls on either side, the western one is the summit. The views – especially of the Mamores – are good, but will get even better.

A grassy ridge snakes onward towards Màm na Gualainn, which from here is somewhat sprawling. The walking is a joy however, with vistas that improve steadily with the ridge's situation. Looking back from below Màm na Gualainn's eastern plateau, Beinn na Caillich is a shapely pyramid, echoed across the trench of Loch Leven in the graceful Corbett of Garbh Bheinn; south of which is the famous arête of the Aonach Eagach. The Aonach Eagach reveals itself only to those prepared to get personal. From distant vantage points it doesn't look particularly special – little more than a crinkly skyline, but today's walk provides one of the best remote views of it, displaying its rough northern corries.

A brief pull up over Màm na Gualainn's shambolic eastern plateau followed by a gentle peat-hagged dip leads to stony slopes below the cropped turf of the broad summit. It isn't the airiest of summits, but the views over Loch Linnhe to the rumpled wilds of Ardgour, above which Garbh Bheinn stands like a castle, are very fine – especially when shafts of sunlight play over the ridges of Beinn a' Bheithir, turning the sea to silver.

From the summit, the mountain's grassy south-west ridge allows height to be shed quickly, without being too hard on the knees. Towards the base it is worthwhile angling northwards to the high point of the neighbouring pass (marked by a huge pile of stones). This provides a final view of the western Mamores and allows an ancient right of way to ease the final part of the descent before it fades in wet heather some way east of the forestry plantation. Marooned halfway down is a Scottish Rights of Way Society signpost. Below it, a path can just be discerned descending into a bracken-filled depression, eventually leading through a gate in a dry-stone wall towards a ruin and small stand of woodland, where a short track leading to the road is picked up.

The return along the lochshore road is undoubtedly easier with a bicycle or second car, but in spite of the tarmac it is usually quiet enough and in sufficiently beautiful surroundings to be a very pleasant walk.

WALK 7
BEINN A' BHEITHIR

Distance: 11km (7 miles). Return along road, 4km (2.5 miles).
Ascent: 1310m (4300ft).
Start: Large car park off A82 in Ballachulish.
Finish: South Ballachulish (GR047591).
Maps: OS Landranger 41 *Ben Nevis, Fort William & surrounding area* or Pathfinder 305 *Glencoe*.
Terrain: A steep and sometimes exposed and rocky ridge with sections of straightforward scrambling is followed by mainly straightforward ridge walking, with a little mild scrambling on the narrow crest of Sgòrr Dhònuill.
Stalking information: No restrictions on access.

Gaelic names
> **Beinn a' Bheithir** (bYn a **vay**heer˙): Mountain of the serpent, or of the thunderbolt.
> **Ballachulish:** From Baile a' Chaolais (ba:la a **cho**:leesh), meaning town of the narrows.
> **Sgòr Bhàn** (skor **vaan**): Pale peak.
> **Sgòrr Dhearg** (skor **yer**ak): Red peak
> **Sgòrr Dhònuill** (skor **ghaw**-il˙): Donald's peak.
> **Sgòrr a' Chaolais** (skor a **cho**:leesh): Peak of the narrows.
> **Gleann a' Chaolais** (glyown a **cho**:leesh): Glen of the narrows.

Caillich Bheithir, the Celtic goddess of winter and death (which at one time were largely interchangeable concepts) was apparently somewhat fickle. While she spent much of her time as an immortally youthful maiden of serenely bewitching beauty, she was also by all accounts healthily in touch with a deep-seated and not inconsiderable anger. This she gave vent to in the guise of an indiscriminately destructive serpentine demon, who was blamed for the majority of unwelcome events of an elemental nature such as floods, storms, gales - and even for moving the odd mountain.

Top: Beinn a' Bheithir from the Western slopes of Màm na Gualainn.

This unfortunate scapegoat for many of the woes of the area was rumoured to inhabit the slopes of Beinn a' Bheithir, a splendid horseshoe of peaks standing guard over the entrance to Loch Leven. Although *beithir* can mean many things, from enormous serpents or flatfish even, to thunderbolts and bears, it is fairly certain that the mountain, which offers some of the finest views covered by this book, takes its name from her.

Unquestionably the finest way up Beinn a' Bheithir for anyone of moderate scrambling ability is via the ENE ridge of Sgòr Bhàn, which rises in one ever steepening sweep above Ballachulish to a steep and narrow crest crossed by steps of slate. In some lights especially this ridge can look quite daunting from the vicinity of Ballachulish, but there is really only one point on it where the scrambling is anything other than very easy.

From Ballachulish, a short road along the west side of the River Laroch leads past a school, becoming a track and then a path which follows an old right of way over into Glen Creran. After a kilometre or so, bear off right, up the hillside. The heather and grass slopes above gradually swell and constrict until they reach the first rocks of Sgòr Bhàn's ENE ridge.

The views are already very fine. Ballachulish was once a large industrial town and, malicious demons aside, most of the local mountain moving activity was conducted by stoneworkers who, from the latter half of the 18th century, excavated the great slateworks clearly visible above the town to the east. These have been extensively re-landscaped, and although the shore of Loch Leven here is now wholly artificial, they are no longer the eyesore they once were. Their impact certainly pales into insignificance beside proposals which have recently been put forward for a superquarry on the other side of Beinn a' Bheithir near Kentallen.

Ballachulish was also a site of an epic battle between the men of the legendary Fingal, one of the greatest Celtic heroes, and 40 longships full of Viking warriors led by King Errigon of Sora. When the Vikings arrived most of Fingal's men, the *Fianna*, were apparently swanning about the hills hunting deer, so Fingal bamboozled them with his clearly remarkable line in humbug until reinforcements arrived.

The resultant stalemate produced a gentleman's agreement that the opposing forces should each put forward 140 of their best men to settle things. After the sixth batches of 140 had butchered each other, the Vikings clearly began to realise that they were facing an even more frightening bunch of nutters than themselves, and the survivors who weren't hewn down in the shallows of Loch Leven fled in two ships, which themselves were soon wrecked. The most

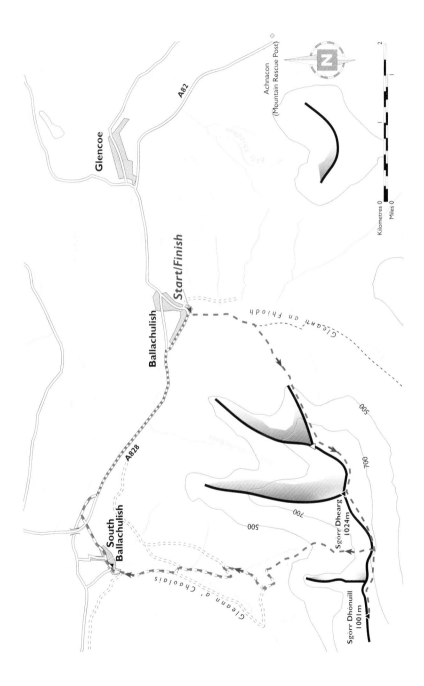

Glencoe

A82

Achnacon
(Mountain Rescue Post)

Start/Finish

Ballachulish

Gleann an Fhiodh

South
Ballachulish

A828

Gleann a' Chaolais

500

700

700

500

Sgorr Dhearg
1024m

Sgorr Dhonuill
1001m

Kilometres 0
Miles 0

important pieces of King Erragon and his followers were respectfully buried at Laroch, which is unfortunately now under rather a lot of slate.

There is no need for detailed description of the ascent to Sgòr Bhàn: just keep climbing until you reach the top. A well developed path winds its way between the smaller outcrops, and the routes up the larger ones are obvious by worn rock and grass. Some of the rock demands care: apparently reliable holds can give way, and there are loose stones and blocks resting on ledges. Soon though, the ridge fades into the crest of Sgòr Bhàn, which is followed without incident to the summit cairn, a superb viewpoint 947m (3104ft) above Loch Leven.

A remarkably graceful ridge curves around to the west and the 1024m (3361ft) Munro of Sgòrr Dhearg, highest peak of Beinn a' Bheithir. The views from here are better still: an unbroken panorama of sea and mountain, and a fine excuse to stop for lunch. Landmarks which are quite distant look strangely near, and Loch Leven – in reality nearly 4km away – seems almost underfoot.

Beinn a' Bheithir and Loch Leven from Stob Coire nam Beith; Glen Coe.

A fairly steep descent to the west gains a gentle bealach at 757m, across which creep the rusted and bent iron posts of an old estate boundary. These and the remains of dry-stone walls can be found crossing or following mountain ridges all over the highlands, testifying to the importance once placed on grazing territory for deer and sheep. Above, Sgòrr Dhònuill presents a ridge of steep grass, growing rockier as it rises, with broken crags on the right above Gleann a' Chaolais. Eventually a levelling is reached where

At the base of Sgòrr Bhàn's East-North-East Ridge with Ballachulish below.

the mountain sends a short spur northwards to Sgòrr a' Chaolais - which appears so prominently horn-like in the views of Beinn a' Bheithir from around North Ballachulish. Above this the ridge becomes narrow and scrambly, the path following the bouldery edge of some quite impressive crags to the worn turf and cairn of the summit at 1001m (3284ft).

It is now possible to continue around the horseshoe over the innumerable rises and hollows of the broad back of Creag Ghorm. However, breaching the forestry around its base is nowhere particularly pleasant, and the comparatively straightforward descent west down the open slopes above Kentallen leaves a lot of narrow and often busy road to cover on the return.

The easiest option is to return to the bealach between the mountain's two highest peaks, and descend through the rough grassland and boulders of the corrie to the north. An obvious path follows a plantation fence northwards before plunging steeply through the trees to the forestry roads of Gleann a' Chaolais, which in turn lead tortuously down to the public road at South Ballachulish. The forestry hereabouts has always been less than subtle, and now that it is being felled and replanted, the basin of Gleann a' Chaolais resembles a moth-eaten patchwork quilt inhabited by bored Royal Engineers, so perhaps the less said about it the better.

The walk back along the busy road to the starting point is, perhaps surprisingly, not unpleasant. There is a roadside pavement for much of the way, with fine views of the Pap of Glen Coe, which on a still, clear evening will be bathed in the rich light of the setting sun shining off Loch Leven.

On the East-North-East ridge of Sgòr Bhàn.

WALK 8

SGÒRR NA CÌCHE
(THE PAP OF GLENCOE)

Distance: 6km (3.5 miles).
Ascent: 740m (2400ft).
Start/finish: Glencoe village: take minor road at the junction of A82 and B863. Parking is available in the village (please park tidily).
Maps: OS Landranger 41 *Ben Nevis, Fort William & surrounding* area or Outdoor Leisure 38 *Ben Nevis & Glencoe* or Pathfinder 305 *Glencoe*. Harveys Walker's Map or Superwalker *Glen Coe*.
Terrain: Easy walking, boggy in places; scrambly near the summit of the mountain.
Stalking information: No restrictions on access.

Gaelic names
> **Sgòrr na Cìche** (skor na **kee**:cha): Peak of the nipple.
> **Sgòrr nam Fiannaidh** (skor nam **fee**anee): Peak of the Fianna.
> **Beinn a' Bheithir** (bYn a **vay**heer): Mountain of the serpent, or of the thunderbolt.
> **Garbh Bheinn** (**gar**av vYn): Rough mountain.
> **Sgor na h-Ulaidh** (skor na **hoo**lee): Peak of the treasure.
> **Eilean Munde** (elyan **moo**nda): Island of Mundus.
> **Glen Coe:** from *gleann comhan* (glyown **co**vanʸ), origin obscure.

This delightful short walk is an excellent introduction to the Glencoe area, and a good choice for a lazy day, or an afternoon or morning clear spell during poor weather (alternatively it can easily be made a finale to the traverse of the Aonach Eagach described in Walk 9). Although the Pap of Glencoe, to use the name popular amongst visitors, reaches a mere 742m (2434ft), just short of Corbett status, it provides an unsurpassed viewpoint for Loch Leven and the sea-loch's surrounding peaks.

Top: Sgòrr na Cìche, Sgòrr nam Fiannaidh and Bidean nam Bian from near Callert.

The pap of Glencoe from Loch Leven.

Park tidily in Glencoe village, where a store is handy for provisions or a drink at the walk's end. From the village cross the bridge over the River Coe and head towards the Clachaig Inn. The road is single-track, overhung with a beautiful dense canopy of broadleaved woodland, and gives very pleasant walking in any weather.

Just under a kilometre after leaving the village, well past a tiny electricity station, two tracks appear on the left. Follow the right hand one up the hillside, turning left when it forks. Almost immediately a small path appears; leading uphill past a small waterworks, along the bank of a stream past a tiny concrete dam, then curving leftwards into a lovely secluded ravine of oak and ash.

Before long, a steep bank of tree-root buttressed earth leads away from the stream to open slopes which, for much of the year, are choked with bracken. Alternatively, all soil-scrambling can be avoided by a wet and intermittent stony path to the right of the main ravine directly above the dammed pool, which skirts the woodland to rejoin the main path.

Indistinct in places, the path leads directly up the hillside alongside a tiny tributary of the stream it has just left, which in summer is a riotous burbling carpet of water plants, lined with purple foxgloves. At a horizontal terrace in the hillside, the stream vanishes into a little marsh. Here the path turns right along the terrace for 100m or so,

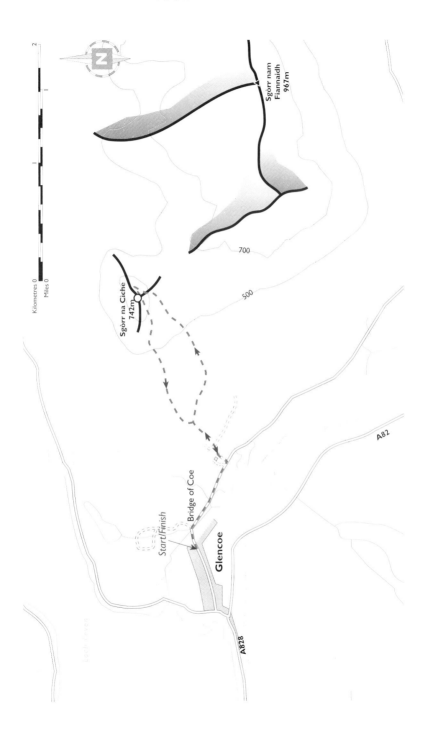

then angles up across the hillside. The ground is soft peat which is eroding badly: a situation that can only worsen until remedial measures are taken.

After approximately 500m the path reaches another ravine, following its left bank directly up the hillside once more. The path zigzags briefly left onto a little heathery ridge before resuming its upwards course along a little grassy vale, past a tiny lochan, emerging at a rocky knoll above the bealach between Sgòrr na Cìche and the much higher Sgòrr nam Fiannaidh: the westmost peak of the Aonach Eagach named after the Fianna, who dug defensive trenches hereabouts during their disagreements with the Vikings under Errigon of Sora.

Now comes the best bit: the climb up the mountain's little summit cone, which rises quite steeply above the shoulder. The path dog-legs left, then climbs steadily rightwards through scree and increasingly rocky terrain (presenting a plethora of short scrambling routes to anyone so inclined) until the ground levels off on the north side of the mountain. Blocks and slabs of light grey quartzite now lead directly to the pleasantly chaotic summit, which is crowned with half a dozen large cairns.

The views are fascinating, both scenically and historically. The finest objectives are graceful Beinn a' Bheithir above the steely ribbon of Loch Leven, and the turrets of distant Garbh Bheinn rising to the west in Ardgour above the mouth of the loch. Spanned by the rather stark Ballachulish bridge, Loch Leven was once one of numerous similar obstacles to movement up and down the west coast of the Highlands. The little Kinlochleven conurbation once thrived on traffic forced around the loch head, but its strategic position was eroded first by the Ballachulish ferries, then the building of the bridge in 1975 – which might have made it a virtual ghost town but for the aluminium works. Its operators, Alcan Smelting and Power UK (formerly the British Aluminium Company and then British Alcan), are due to leave before long but bold plans to revitalise the village, based on tourism and outdoor recreation, are being formulated.

The Aonach Eagach hides behind Sgòrr nam Fiannaidh, which is not inspiring from here, but there is a fine perspective of Sgòr na h-Ulaidh to the south. Obvious in Loch Leven is Eilean Munde, with its ruined church, which was used until 1653. This tiny, partly wooded island was settled briefly around 600 AD by St Mundus, an Irish disciple of St Columba who came here from Iona, and for centuries the island was the religious centre for the region. Free from the scavenging wolves which once roamed the mainland, it was also a burial ground shared by local clans including the MacDonalds of Glencoe. Although the persecuted Scottish wolf was finally made extinct in the 18th century, burials here continued.

Sgòrr na Cìche also of course overlooks the scene of the 1692 massacre of Glencoe MacDonalds, when, under orders from the government of King William III in London, two companies of soldiers who had for ten days been enjoying the customary hospitality of the MacDonalds, turned on their hosts during a blizzard in the early hours of 13 February, killing 38, mainly at Invercoe, Inverigan and Achnacon, while 300 escaped into the hills, some to perish from exposure.

Following a piece of investigative journalism by an Irishman, Charles Leslie, the massacre became a political scandal. Though similar tragedies litter Highland history (albeit seldom involving such levels of government-sanctioned treachery), the Glencoe massacre has become pre-eminent, along with the crushing defeat of the 1745-46 Jacobite rebellion at the battle of Culloden and its long, painful aftermath – including, eventually, the infamous clearances, when the land was emptied of people in favour of sheep, forcing mass emigration to North America and Australia. As much as the scenery, it is the massacre, or a romantic notion of it, which has made the glen world famous. A commemorative ceremony is held each February, on the anniversary, at the memorial in Glencoe village.

For those with a taste for easy scrambling the most interesting descent is westwards, following cairns down a broad, slabby ridge to a scrambly path descending a steepish rocky section. The path continues zigzagging down, negotiating the narrowest point of a

Beinn a' Bheithir and Loch Leven from the Pap of Glencoe.

boulderfield and alternating between rocks, scree and heather until easier-angled peat moorland (blaeberries in late summer) is reached below. The path, followed directly down into another heathery ravine, alternates between sphagnum and peat. Though becoming increasingly eroded, it gives good views back to the Pap.

The ravine steepens, trees become visible in it, and a distinct path bears off to the left. After descending briefly through the bracken, this follows a little ridge contouring the hillside, soon rejoining the path taken on the way up, which is followed back to the road and Bridge of Coe.

The Pap of Glencoe from the south-east..

THE AONACH EAGACH

Distance: 8.5km (5.5 miles).
Ascent: 1190m (3900ft).
Start: A82, 500m west of Allt na-reigh (GR174567).
Finish: 1km NW of Leacantuim (GR113584).
Maps: OS Landranger 41 *Ben Nevis, Fort William & surrounding area* or Outdoor Leisure 38 *Ben Nevis & Glencoe* or Pathfinder 305 *Glencoe*. Harveys Walker's Map or Superwalker *Glen Coe*.
Terrain: The ridge itself involves inescapable medium-grade scrambling which is exposed, quite sustained, and often slippery – requiring confidence, a good head for heights, and scrambling experience. A precautionary rope and the company of someone who knows how to use it are advised for less confident parties.
Stalking Information: The walk is mostly on ground owned by The National Trust for Scotland, and there are no restrictions on access.

Gaelic names
    Aonach Eagach (oe:noch **e**goch): Notched ridge.
    Am Bodach (am **bo**toch): The old man.
    Sgòrr nam Fiannaidh (skor nam **fee**anee): Peak of the Fianna.
    Meall Dearg (myowl **dye**rak): Red mound.
    Stob Coire Lèith (stob kora **lay**): Peak of the grey corrie.
    Allt Ruigh (owlt **roo**ee): Stream of the outstretched mountain
        base or summer shieling.
    Aonach Dubh (oe:noch **doo**): Dark ridge.
    Sròn Garbh (strawn **gar**av): Rough nose.
    Bidean nam Bian (beedyan nam **byown**). Probably from
        Bidean nam Beann, meaning peak of the mountains.

The Aonach Eagach is probably the most famous ridge scramble in Scotland: and not without reason. Few routes outside the Cuillin of Skye rival its combination of sustained interest and difficulty, situation and exposure, and none that do are so readily accessible from the populous lands of the south.

Top: The Aonach Eagach above Glen Coe from the north end of Beinn Fhada (note the hang-glider).

This popularity is not without problems of course, and there are now days in summer when the Aonach Eagach is so overcrowded that some mountain guides will go nowhere near it. The ridge itself stretches for 3km between the 943m (3085ft) Top of Am Bodach and the 967m (3173ft) Munro of Sgòrr nam Fiannaidh, taking in another Munro – 953m (3118ft) Meall Dearg – and a second Top, 940m (3080ft) Stob Coire Lèith, on the way. Though technically moderate, the scrambling is sometimes quite daunting, requiring a well developed head for heights – and confidence, for the only safe descents into Glen Coe are from either end.

A word of warning: in Glen Coe the number of accidents in relation to the number of visits is much higher than in other areas. This should speak for itself, but approached sensibly, a traverse of the Aonach Eagach should be an enjoyable and memorable experience.

The best direction for the traverse is east to west. This way the initial ascent is shorter and far more interesting, and the trickiest step on the ridge – which can be unnerving for the uninitiated if downclimbed – is tackled uphill. From a small car-park at the bend in the A82 just west of the cottages of Allt-na-reigh, a good path climbs a grassy spur below Am Bodach. It climbs above the Allt Ruigh for a short way before veering leftwards again, giving stunning perspectives of the great hanging valleys and rocky spurs of Bidean nam Bian opposite, and Loch Achtriochtan nestling between towering Aonach Dubh and the gully-seamed flank of the Aonach Eagach.

There is some truth in Glen Coe's reputation for gloominess: on a dreich day especially, the enclosing flanks and walls certainly make their presence felt in a way shared by few other places in these islands, but on a clear, sunny day, it is a place of colour, light and space. The National Trust for Scotland, which bought the glen in the 1930s, has been criticised for installing footbridges and car-parks against the wishes of the late Percy Unna, whose funding made the purchase possible. However, the Trust is spending hundreds of thousands of pounds on both conservation work and footpath repair in the glen, so perhaps we should not be too critical.

Curving back around a rocky nose, the path climbs into a gorge-like corrie, and steadily up its more open headwall to emerge at a bealach between the dumpy Sròn Garbh and Am Bodach. A clamber of 130m through quite rough ground then leads to Am Bodach's flattish 943m (3085ft) summit. The ridge which follows is a magical mystery tour: the route so intricate, yet so obvious, that a concise description is both near-impossible and unnecessary. Besides, if in doubt, there will probably be hordes of other scramblers to follow.

A brief description of prominent features however may be helpful. The first obstacle of note is only briefly west of the cairn: an

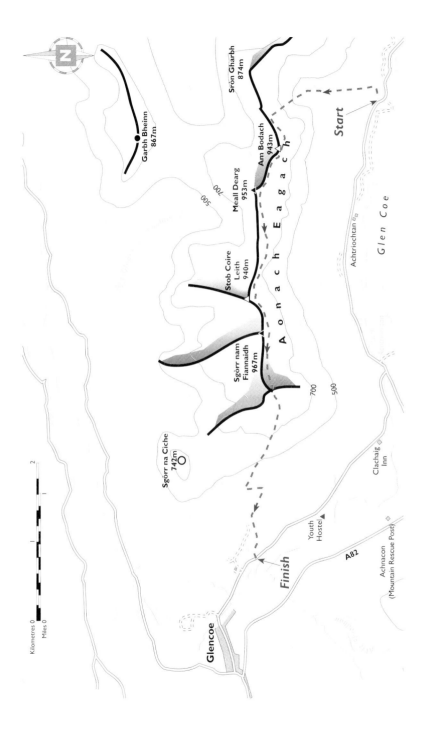

Garbh Bheinn
867m

Srón Gharbh
874m

Am Bodach
943m

Meall Dearg
953m

700

500

Stob Coire
Leith
940m

A o n a c h   E a g a c h

Sgòrr nam
Fiannaidh
967m

700

500

Sgòrr na Ciche
742m

Start

Glen Coe

Achtriochtan

Clachaig
Inn

Youth
Hostel

Achnacon
(Mountain Rescue Post)

A82

Finish

Glencoe

Kilometres 0
Miles 0

2

The Aonach Eagach from Loch Achtriochtan, Glen Coe.

alarmingly sudden drop, descended on polished steps of rock. Following various entertaining shenanigans involving arêtes, chimneys and suchlike, its crest rises more easily to the 953m (3085ft) summit of Meall Dearg. This peak was immortalised as the last Munro of the first ever Munroist, the Reverend A.E. Robertson – Sir Hugh Munro himself having narrowly failed to complete them. It is gleefully recorded that Robertson kissed first the cairn and then his wife, but frustratingly no mention is made of her response.

The views from the entire ridge are superb, and it is well worth saving the traverse for a good day. Glen Coe owes much of its spectacular nature to the same process which shaped Ben Nevis in the same geological period roughly 400 billion years ago, and is a world famous example of cauldron subsidence in ancient rocks.

Once again a cone-shaped plug of metamorphic rocks and lavas – this time 10km wide – sagged over 600m into a chamber of molten rock, creating a circular surface depression (caldera) and intense volcanic activity. Subsided lava flows of varying mineral compositions can now be seen banding the spurs of Bidean nam Bian opposite.

Onwards, the ridge looks mouth-watering. Crenellated into crooked teeth, it swoops around below the pointed Stob Coire Lèith, before kinking back again towards the graceful Sgòrr nam Fiannaidh. There are dozens of entertaining bits on this section, but the highlight is the 'Crazy Pinnacles': several fingers of rock sitting squarely astride one of the very narrowest parts of the ridge, which are best tackled directly. Immediately beyond them comes the hardest two metres on the ridge: an awkward and traffic-polished slabby step which feels, briefly, like rock-climbing. This is no place for a slip.

Beyond are the 'teeth' so obvious from Meall Dearg, which prove easy by comparison. The cairn of 940m (3080ft) Stob Coire Lèith marks the end of the difficulties, and mainly easy walking leads to the cairn, trig pillar and stone windbreak capping the bald domed summit of 967m (3173ft) Sgòrr nam Fiannaidh. From here, head west to a small, broad subsidiary summit.

There is a path (I use the term loosely) descending from Sgòrr nam Fiannaidh directly to the Clachaig Inn, but this is only for masochists with a death wish, comprising loose scree and unstable boulders poised above a yawning declivity, namely the Clachaig Gully. At 530m, this famous gully is the longest in Scotland. Its first ascent by the legendary W.H. Murray along with A.M. McAlpine, J.K.W. Dunn and W.G. Marskell is vividly described in Murray's *Mountaineering in Scotland*, a book written from memory in a German prisoner of war camp, which has become a mountaineering bible.

The recommended method of retreat is to head due west to a broad subsidiary summit, and bear down its north-west slopes. On a good day the views over Loch Leven are unforgettable, made all the better by the knowledge of having completed such a magnificent mountain route. An increasingly well defined path slants down the hillside, joining another de-scending from the bealach between the Pap of Glencoe from Sgòrr nam Fiannaidh. After zigzagging through the heather, this descends beside a ravine to the old road between Bridge of Coe and the Clachaig Inn, which follows the line of the 1785 military road through the glen.

If walking the 7km back to the day's starting point, there is at least the mountaineers' bar of the Clachaig Inn to break the journey. The A82 can be unpleasant walking, but fortunately its line, established from 1929-31, differs from that of the old road, which can now be followed in peace for much of the way back.

Scrambling in solitude on the Crazy Pinnacles.

THE TOPS OF BIDEAN NAM BIAN

Distance: 11.5km (7 miles).
Ascent: 1585m (5200ft).
Start: Car park by bridge on A82 near Achnambeithach (GR138566).
Finish: Layby on A82 by waterfalls (GR183563).
Maps: OS Landranger 41 *Ben Nevis, Fort William & surrounding area* or Outdoor Leisure 38 *Ben Nevis & Glencoe* or Pathfinder 305 *Glencoe*. Harveys Walker's Map or Superwalker *Glen Coe*.
Terrain: High level ridge-walking, mostly rocky with low-grade scrambling in places, and a brief section of harder scrambling on the descent to Beinn Fhada. Some loose sections and the final descent require care.
Stalking information: The walk described is all on ground owned by The National Trust for Scotland, and there are no restrictions on access.

Gaelic names

    Bidean nam Bian (beedyan nam **byown**): Probably from *Bidean nam Beann*, meaning peak of the mountains.

    Stob Coire nan Lochan (stob kora nan **loch**an): Peak of the corrie of the little lochs.

    Aonach Dubh (oe:noch **doo**): Dark ridge.

    Geàrr Aonach (**gyaar** oe:noch): Short ridge.

    Beinn Fhada (bYn **ata**): Long mountain.

    Stob Coire nam Beith (stob kora nam **bay**): Peak of the corrie of the birches.

    Stob Coire Sgreamhach (stob kora **skray**voch): Peak of the fearful/dreadful corrie.

    Allt Coire nam Beithach (owlt kora nam **bay**hoch): Stream of the corrie of the birches.

    Coire nam Beithach (kora nam **bay**hoch): Corrie of the birches.

Top: Bidean nam Bian from near Callert.

An t-Sròn (an **trawn**): The nose.
Coire nan Lochan (kora nan **lo**chan): Corrie of the little lochs.
Coire Gabhail (kora **ga**vayl): Corrie of the booty (namely, pilfered cattle!).

At 1150m (3766ft) Bidean nam Bian is the highest mountain in the old county of Argyll, and regarded by many as one of Scotland's finest. It is a complex miniature massif of high rocky ridges, spectacular faces and buttresses which have produced some of the finest summer and winter climbing in these islands, and deeply gouged valleys and corries possessing an atmosphere of seclusion which is remarkable given their proximity to the A82 trunk road.

Glen Coe owes much of its uniquely brooding character to the looming cragginess of Bidean nam Bian, though the summit is largely hidden. It lurks behind the famous 'Three Sisters' of Aonach Dubh, Geàrr Aonach and Beinn Fhada – glacially truncated spurs of impressive rocky steepness which stand sentinel over the glen – and the graceful pyramid of Stob Coire nan Lochan, rearing over the sisters like a stern matriarch, and often mistaken for the main summit itself.

Though the easiest routes to the summit involve only mild scrambling, Bidean nam Bian is still a comparatively serious mountain, finding a safe descent being far more critical than on all but a handful of mainland Scottish peaks. Many inexperienced parties have first felt fear lost in the clouds on its ridges, but to enjoy her at her best, all 'Bidean' needs is a little respect.

Beside the bridge over the River Coe a kilometre east of the Clachaig Inn, a tiny kissing gate leads to a narrow path winding southwards up the hillside in the shadow of Aonach Dubh. Once eroding badly, this path has now been restored. Long sections higher up are beautifully pitched: stones gathered from the surrounding hillsides laid like cobbles into the ground and wedged by hammering smaller stones into the cracks, which soon become silted up and vegetated. Some argue that pitched paths are intrusively artificial, as well as horribly slippery in the wet, but the fact is that in Scottish conditions pitching seems the only effective solution to the demands made of routes as popular as this one.

The lava cliffs of Aonach Dubh overhead begin to look like castle battlements, with the dripping gash of No 6 Gully, a classic winter ice route, obvious on the right. The path negotiates a short, wet scrambly section above the Allt Coire nam Beithach, followed by some scree and close views of the fine waterfall so obvious from the glen below. Stob Coire nam Beith's rugged 460m north face bursts into view as the path enters the jaws of Coire nam Beithach.

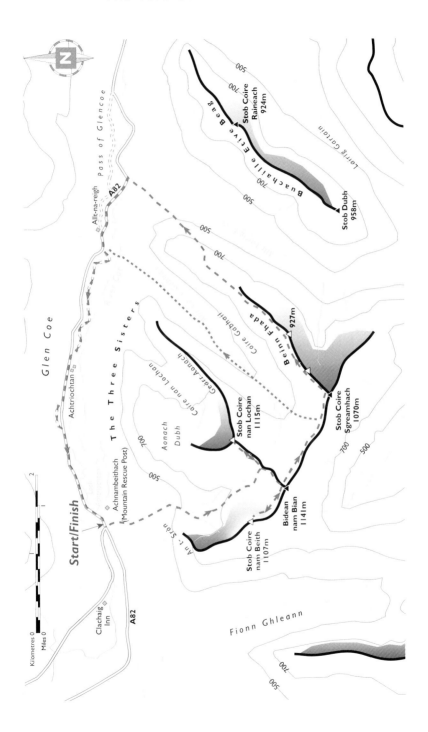

Coire Gabhail and Beinn Fhada from below Stob Coire Sgreamhach.

The stream draining the corrie is followed for a couple of hundred metres, then crossed: first by boulders below a 4m waterfall, then again where a tributary joins from the right. Here the path loses its sense of purpose. Strike uphill to the right of the main stream until a path again becomes obvious, climbing scree and a scrambly rock band to an untidy cairn on a ridge of glacially smoothed rock, which gives a fine view of Coire nam Beithach's gloomily impressive architecture.

The ridge leads up rightwards to a path. This climbs up the corrie through screes below the north face of Stob Coire nam Beith, before crossing the corrie floor to follow the stream again. From here Stob Coire nam Beith is a confusion of pink rock. The path reaches the barrier of a *roche moutonnée* – a glacial landform created where pressure-induced melting of ice on the uphill side of a rock outcrop let water, under enormous pressure beneath the glacier, scour the rock smooth; while the pressure decrease on the downhill side allowed frost-shattering and freezing of loosened blocks to the glacier's underside, producing a plucked, stepped face. The path climbs easily up these steps.

Having crossed a branch of the shrinking stream, the path weaves up a grassy ridge in the shadow of the twin Diamond and Church Door Buttresses to the upper corrie, which is spectacularly carpeted with brightly coloured mosses. From here Church Door Buttress, home to some of the best mountain rock-climbs in Scotland, resembles a huge barrel. Beyond a chaos of angular boulders, an obvious path snakes up red screes and grey rock bands left of Diamond Buttress to the bealach between Stob Coire nan Lochan and Bidean nam Bian.

This ascent is not quite as unpleasant as it looks, and the view from the bealach (which sports particularly comfortable chair-shaped rocks), over a peppering of lochans to the Rannoch Moor peaks, is as sudden as it is welcome. Stob Coire nan Lochan beckons. A straightforward detour, its rocky 1115m (3657ft) summit provides bird's eye views of the other Glen Coe summits and the columnar cliffs of Coire nan Lochain, one of the busiest winter climbing grounds in the country.

The climb to Bidean nam Bian is rocky and, especially just above the bealach, quite steep, with some optional mild scrambling. Considering its massive appearance, Bidean has a surprisingly pointed summit – and even finer views. The Aonach Eagach actually looks rather small: above it rise the steel-grey Mamores and the brooding hulk of Ben Nevis, which is not at its best from here. Westwards, Beinn a' Bheithir rises splendidly above lochs Leven and Linnhe, and south is a superb prospect of Loch Etive, flanked majestically by bens Starav and Cruachan.

The horizons are less expansive from 1107m (3621ft) Stob Coire nam Beith, 750m to the NW, but this detour is worth it for a vertiginous view down to the walk's starting point in Glen Coe. Having returned to the main summit, prepare for a knee-grinding descent ESE to the base of Stob Coire Sgreamhach.

From here it is possible to descend, by a steep earthy gully, into Coire Gabhail – also known as the Lost Valley. This hanging glacial trench, screened from Glen Coe by woods and the boulders of an ancient rockfall from Gearr Aonach, is a stunning place, especially when lingering snow patches lend the peaks at its head an Alpine character. Though solitude is hard to find here in summer now, it is easy to see how the MacDonalds of Glen Coe used it for hiding their – and other people's – cattle.

Descending Coire Gabhail is a sensible shorter option for anyone unsure of the scrambling or tricky final descent awaiting on Beinn Fhada. If embracing the challenge, however, climb to 1072m (3497ft) Stob Coire Sgreamhach: very rocky in its top part, with fine views back to Bidean. It was elevated to Munro status in summer 1997. From the summit descend steeply NW, slightly right of the ridge crest, always keeping right to avoid difficulties. Towards the bottom the ridge becomes quite narrow and scrambly, suddenly disclosing a steep 30m rock step which provides an entertaining scramble to a neck above earthy gullies.

A pleasant stroll now gains the finest and, at 952m (3116ft), highest summit on the undulating ridge of Beinn Fhada; 500m of further excellent walking leads to a second Top. From here the ridge descends gradually over knolly rises and outcrops, with magnificent views of Coire Gabhail.

As the ridge steepens into its craggy nose overlooking Glen Coe (which provides the best views of the Aonach Eagach from anywhere but the Aonach itself), pick the easiest-looking line down the broken hillside to the east; trending northwards but keeping sufficiently south to avoid the crags. A faint path can be picked up, eventually descending a shallow northwards-slanting earth and scree gully walled to the left by a small crag, below which a grassy scoop leads to moorland and the Allt Làirig Eilde. On a hot day, a dip in some slot-like pools above the roadside waterfalls is a fitting finale.

For those without transport, the 5km stroll back down Glen Coe along the old road amid such glorious scenery more than makes up for the short unavoidable sections of the A82.

Gorge in Coire Gabhail.

WALK 11

SGOR NA H-ULAIDH

Distance: 12km (7.5 miles).
Ascent: 1100m (3600ft).
Start/Finish: A82 near Achnacon (GR118565).
Maps: OS Landranger 41 *Ben Nevis, Fort William & surrounding area* or Outdoor Leisure 38 *Ben Nevis & Glencoe* or Pathfinder 305 *Glencoe*. Harveys Walker's Map and Superwalker *Glen Coe*.
Terrain: Fairly straightforward ridge walking after a mildly scrambly ascent, though descent east of the main summit requires care in poor visibility. There is a track and a good path up the glen, but subsequent ground is largely pathless.
Stalking Information: Glenleacnamuide Estate, tel 01855 811311.

Gaelic names
  Sgor na h-Ulaidh (skor na **hoo**lee): Peak of the treasure.
  Gleann Leac na Muidhe (glyow lyechk na **moo**ya): Glen of the
    slab of the churn.
  Allt na Muidhe (owlt na **moo**ya): Stream of the churn.
  Meall Lighiche (myowl **lyee**-eecha): Doctor's peak.
  Beinn Fhionnlaidh (bYn **yoon**lY): Finlay's mountain.
  Stob an Fhuarain (stob an **oo**-aran): Peak of the spring.
  Aonach Dubh a' Ghlinne (oe:noch doo a **ghlee**:nya): Dark
    ridge of the glens.

The Munro of Sgòr na h-Ulaidh is not the most prominent of the mountains of Glen Coe, crouching in shy isolation at the head of the quiet Gleann Leac na Muidhe as though resigned to neglect in favour of its more ego-strutting neighbours to the east. Despite its retiring nature and lack of prominent features, however, it is a rough and steep mountain which might have received considerable attention if situated elsewhere.

This is a walk to savour when Bidean nam Bian or the Aonach Eagach seem too serious, or the mood arises for something a little quieter, as of all the Glen Coe peaks, Sgòr na h-Ulaidh is the most

Top: Sgòr na h-Ulaidh from below Stob an Fhuarain.

Sgòr na h-Ulaidh from upper Gleann Leac na Muidhe.

likely to offer solitude. Approached in this way, its ascent by the described route should be a pleasure.

The walk starts on the A82 at the turn-off of the track up Gleann Leac na Muidhe, a hundred metres east of which is a car park. Once past a gate and cattle grid, the gravel track winds along the glen for a little over a kilometre below the dumpy Meall Mòr before swinging close to the boisterous Allt na Muidhe, crossing it by a wooden bridge and entering a small stand of conifers.

Among them is a tiny white-painted corrugated cottage, and nearby a luxurious new house. The track continues to the self-catering Glencoe Mountain Cottages at Gleann-leac-na-muidhe. A short way beyond are farm buildings, above which lie the ruins of the summer shieling of MacIan, the elderly chief of the MacDonald clan killed in the massacre of 1692. It has been claimed that he perished here, but with heavy snow at the time it is much more likely the old man was enjoying the warmth of his home in Invercoe. Whatever the location, he was shot in the back while rising from his bed, and his wife was so badly knocked about that she also died. The track turns the buildings on the right through two gates, after which the terrain starts to open out.

A final gate below another elongated scrap of forestry marks the end of the track and the start of the wilder upper glen. A sign requests use of the neighbouring stile. The glen kinks leftwards, giving the first good view of Sgòr na h-Ulaidh, its rugged face cleaved by the gashes of Red Gully (below a curious little nick on the skyline) and the more easy-angled Vixen Gully, both good winter climbs. The path onwards is often boggy, crossing ditch-furrowed ground to a green sward beside the Allt na Muidhe, whose bank it follows between looming grassed-over beds of glacial rubble.

The Allt na Muidhe steepens, creating some lovely pools. As the terrain opens out once more below the crags of Meall Lighiche, the now faint and far drier path crosses the stream, rising up the rim of the great trench it has carved through the terminal moraines of Sgòr na h-Ulaidh's northern corrie. Having gained roughly 100m in height, traverse diagonally up below the mountain's north face to the foot of some steep ground above the bealach separating Sgòr na h-Ulaidh from Meall Lighiche.

Here, rusting boundary posts signal the start of the easiest and most pleasant way up. A rising rightwards traverse up steep, stone-strewn slopes eventually gains a blunt west-facing ridge high above the scraggy plantations of the perfectly U-shaped upper Glen Creran. From here, head straight upwards.

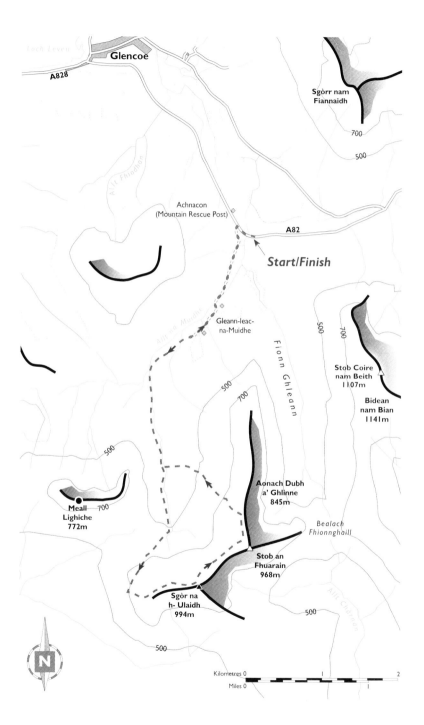

Southwards looms the hump of Beinn Fhionnlaidh - an interesting mountain of sterile quartzite and fertile schist, notable for its flora and unusually good views of Beinn Sgulaird. Above, the ridge grows increasingly steep, with plenty of possibilities for scrambling devotees, although scrambling can be largely avoided by keeping right of the rockiest ground until lines of weakness regain the blunt crest.

With no warning at all the ridge suddenly becomes a level grassy walkway leading to the pinkish stony humps of the summit, still half a kilometre away. Boundary posts are rejoined just before a brief steep rise up an earthy path to the mountain's lofty summit spine. After a brief dip, this leads to the cairn, perched at 994m (3258ft) on a little prow over the edge of the northern crags.

Sgòr na h-Ulaidh is a very fine viewpoint. Not only are the perspectives of the jostling peaks of Glen Coe and the more serene summits of Glen Etive and Appin very good (if slightly censored by the uncompromising bulk of Bidean nam Bian); they are not clichéd. From the summit a short rock step descends to a bed of startlingly red felsite gravel at the top of Red Gully.

Once highly volcanically active, the Glen Coe and Lochaber area is riddled with dykes – intrusions of once molten (igneous) rock forced from plutons through weaknesses in the surrounding rocks. Gullies often owe their existence to these becoming exposed at the surface and proving less resistant to weathering than their surroundings. The felsite of Red Gully is a good example, as are some of the 'notches' of the Aonach Eagach. Another common origin is the crumbling and fracture of rock along lines of movement: faults, such as those down which the Glen Coe caldera sank, an example of which is the Chasm of An t-Sròn above Achnambeithach.

The summit ridge is followed briefly east until a path bears leftwards down steep ground to the bealach between Sgòr na h-Ulaidh and its only Top; 968m (3160ft) Stob an Fhuarain. This is an easy ascent, with good views back to Sgòr na h-Ulaidh. From the summit of Stob an Fhuarain, a wide knolly ridge descends to a short dip before the broad back of Aonach Dubh a' Ghlinne. The undulations of this ridge can prove aggravating, and there are fences around its base, so it is probably best to just descend directly back to Gleann Leac na Muidhe.

Taking a north-west slanting line through initially wet and steep ground allows a grassy ridge above the largest ravine cleaving Aonach Dubh a' Ghlinne's western slopes to be followed easily (knees may disagree!) to the glen. Here, the path is regained and followed back to the road.

The head of Glen Creran from the western ridge of Sgòr na h-Ulaidh.

WALK 12

BUACHAILLE ETIVE MÒR

Distance: 14km (8.6 miles), or 5.5km (3.5 miles) returning via Coire na Tulaich.
Ascent: 1080m (3540ft), or 750m (2500ft) returning via Coire na Tulaich.
Start/finish: Altnafeadh (GR222563) on A82. Usually plenty of car parking available, though the area can fill up early on busy summer weekends.
Maps: OS Landranger 41 *Ben Nevis, Fort William & surrounding area* or Outdoor Leisure 38 *Ben Nevis & Glencoe* or Pathfinders 305 *Glencoe* and 306 *Central Rannoch Moor.* Harveys Walker's Map or Superwalker *Glen Coe.*
Terrain: Sensational and sustained middle-grade scrambling on Curved Ridge (technically slightly more demanding than the Aonach Eagach), which for the inexperienced may necessitate a rope and an experienced colleague. The ascent by Coire na Tulaich involves only very mild scrambling. If descending by Coire na Tulaich, care is needed locating the descent into the corrie in poor visibility. The complete traverse of all the summits of the mountain is a grand and straightforward ridge-walk, followed by a stroll down a graceful glen.
Stalking Information: Once past Lagangarbh, the walk is entirely on land owned by the National Trust for Scotland. No access restrictions.

Gaelic names
> **Buachaille Etive Mòr** (boo-ucheelya etiv **moa:r**): Big herdsman of Etive.
> **Stob Dearg** (stob **dye**rak): Red peak.
> **Coire na Tulaich** (kora na **too**:lich): Corrie of the knoll.
> **Coire Cloiche Finne** (kora clo-eecha **fin**-ya): Corrie of the white stone.
> **Stob na Doire** (stob na **do**ra): Peak of the copse.

Top: Buachaille Etive Mòr at sunset.

Stob Coire Altruim (stob kora **al**trim): Peak of the corrie of nursing/rearing (of deer calves).
Stob na Bròige (stob na **braw**eeka): Peak of the shoe.

Buachaille Etive Mòr is one of the most photographed mountains in Scotland. Little wonder: a regal cone of piled buttresses of pinkish volcanic rhyolite rising in one unbroken sweep from the flatness of Rannoch Moor, it is certainly one of the most spectacular to be visible in all its glory from a well-used trunk road. Its profoundly craggy nature has long made it a favourite haunt of climbers, who swarm over its intricate array of walls and gullies on any good weekend.

Perhaps contrary to its formidable appearance, however, there are several easy routes up the mountain. The trade-route up Coire na Tulaich is just a rough walk – with a surprisingly small ascent of only 750m at that, and it is even possible for those with scrambling experience to breach the highest part of the great eastern crags, by the superb scramble of Curved Ridge.

What is widely known affectionately as 'the Buachaille' is in fact strictly only Stob Dearg, terminal peak of a serpentine ridge linking four summits above 914m (3000ft), which, combined, make up Buachaille Etive Mòr. Together, these give a superb day's walking that does full justice to the mountain.

There is a good view of Curved Ridge from the roadside on the A82 about a kilometre west of the Glen Etive turnoff, and if intending to climb it, a preview of its topography might be advantageous. The face of Stob Dearg is dominated by the squat, bulging North Buttress, directly below the summit. Immediately left of this is the deep gash of Crowberry Gully (the most famous winter climb on the Buachaille), bounded on its left by the well-defined Crowberry Ridge, which sweeps up into the obvious bell-shaped Crowberry Tower.

Left again, less well defined than Crowberry Gully, is Easy Gully. Left of this is a rib of rock kinking rightwards above its rather vague base below Crowberry Ridge, becoming narrower and better defined with height before forming the skyline left of Crowberry Tower. This is Curved Ridge. Some way below it, a conspicuous large slab with a stream cascading over it – the Waterslide Slab – marks the start of the climb to the ridge.

At Altnafeadh vehicles can (at the time of writing) be parked along a lay-by and bumpy track leading to the bridge over the River Coupall. Beyond is the Scottish Mountaineering Club cottage of Lagangarbh. The path past the cottage was once a quagmire, but has been reconstructed and is now generally dry. About 500m from Alltnafeadh it bifurcates, the right fork ascending in an almost straight line into Coire na Tulaich.

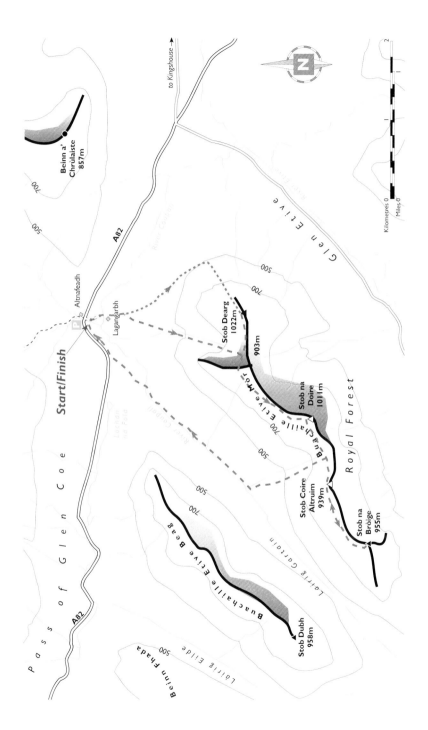

The left fork makes a gradual rising traverse towards the foot of Stob Dearg's east face, gaining height with remarkable ease. The path is pitched in places, negotiating the loose bouldery beds of several gully outflows before eventually crossing the stream pouring off the Waterslide Slab. This is where the fun begins, the path rising beyond the slab first on loose scree, then through intricate and increasingly scrambly broken rocky ground.

A detailed description may confuse rather than illuminate, as the route is logical provided care is taken to follow the most clearly polished rock and the most obvious paths through scree and heather sections. Eventually, beneath the towering base of Crowberry Ridge, the junction of Easy Gully and Crowberry Gully is reached. Curved Ridge begins on the left: a prominent rough rib of shattered rock which develops into an exhilarating scramble up glorious flake and jug-handle holds.

Buachaille Etive Mòr from Beinn a' Chrùlaiste.

On most weekends the air echoes to the shouts and ringing metal of rock-climbers prostrated on Rannoch Wall – the slabby reddish precipice which forms the southern side of Crowberry Ridge above Easy Gully. The easy mid-section of Curved Ridge is often festooned with scramblers captivated by the colourful antics opposite, of which there is a remarkable view: the classic *Agag's Groove* and *January Jigsaw* at the right-hand side of the wall – surprisingly easy climbs given their spectacular nature – usually have parties on them. Curved Ridge is the main descent route for climbers on the wall, so do not be alarmed to find lunatics wearing harnesses and offensively coloured tights jogging nonchalantly down it: a potentially serious threat to a scrambler's pride.

The most exacting part of Curved Ridge is the often steep and exposed upper half. Although a century of traffic (Curved Ridge was first climbed in 1896) has removed most of the loose rock, it has also left what remains very polished. This makes it slippery, but provides a guide to the best line which is more reliable than any guidebook description. The crux is a steep little wall, breached by an extremely polished clamber up a little cleft, on holds that are not particularly positive.

A cairn marks the end of the ridge. From here, climb the right side of the imminent scree gully, and continue up rightwards round the base of Crowberry Tower to the gap between the tower and the rest of Stob Dearg. A sharp scramble out of the gap leads to easier slopes, and finally the 1022m (3345ft) summit, which gives fine views – although not as spectacular as from Curved Ridge. South-west, the Buachaille's crest of Tops recedes gracefully towards Glen Etive.

The easier approach via Coire na Tulaich crosses the burn draining the corrie and follows it up through some rough and wild scenery. A scree slope below the corrie headwall leads to a

Buachaille Etive Mòr from near Altnafeadh.

narrowing gully, avoided by a path which winds up a series of rubble-piled ledges to its right, emerging on a stony bealach a little over 500m west of the summit cairn. If returning by the same route, care should be taken locating this descent in poor visibility, as the surrounding headwall is loose and craggy. The slopes above Coire na Tulaich provide excellent views of Buachaille Etive Beag and the Glen Coe peaks to the west.

From the bealach between Coire na Tulaich and Coire Cloiche Finne to the south (an easy descent to Glen Etive), the Buachaille's stony spine curls south-west again over a minor hump, and up to the graceful 1011m (3316ft) Top of Stob na Doire. Onwards, the ridge dips to a bealach at 815m, then rises stonily again to the craggy 939m (3065ft) Stob Coire Altruim.

It may be worth leaving rucksacks here, as the 2km detour to 955m (3120ft) Stob na Bròige – newly promoted to Munro status in summer 1997, and giving splendid views down Glen Etive – involves minimal descent and reascent, and by far the easiest way off the ridge and back to the day's starting point is to return to the low point between Stob na Doire and Stob Coire Altruim, from where a path leads down the corrie to the north.

After a knee-jarring 450m descent, this crosses the headwaters of the River Coupall to join the well developed path down the Làirig Gartain to the A82. A loop of the old road followed by half a kilometre of tarmac leads back to Altnafeadh.

WALK 13

BUACHAILLE ETIVE BEAG

Distance: 11km (7 miles).
Ascent: 830m (2720ft).
Start/finish: Car park on A82 at foot of Làirig Gartain (GR213560).
Maps: OS Landranger 41 *Ben Nevis, Fort William & surrounding area* or Outdoor Leisure 38 *Ben Nevis & Glencoe* or Pathfinders 305 *Glencoe* and 306 *Central Rannoch Moor*. Harveys Walker's Map or Superwalker *Glen Coe*.
Terrain: A steep initial ascent (optional) calling for routefinding and moderate scrambling ability, followed by straightforward walking on an increasingly airy ridge, and a straightforward descent.
Stalking information: The walk is entirely on land owned by the National Trust for Scotland. No access restrictions.

Gaelic names

> **Buachaille Etive Beag** (boo-ucheelya etiv **bayk**): Little herdsman of Etive.
> **Stob nan Cabar** (stob nan **kap**ar): Peak of the antlers.
> **Lochan na Fola** (lochan na **fo**-la): Little loch of blood.
> **Stob Coire Raineach** (stob kora **ra**nyach): Peak of the fern corrie.
> **Stob Dubh** (stob **doo**): Dark peak.
> **Làirig Èilde** (la:reek **hay**:ltya): Pass of the hind.
> **Làirig Gartain** (La:reek **gar**stan^y): Pass of the tick.
> **Sròn na Làirig** (strawn na **la**:reek): Nose of the pass.

Buachaille Etive Beag, as its name suggests, is very much the little brother of neighbouring Buachaille Etive Mòr, whose proud ramparts are mirrored in the smaller crags of Stob nan Cabar. On closer inspection these prove something of an imposter, of more botanical than rock-climbing interest – but for walkers the 'wee Buachaille' is, in its own way, every bit as good as

Top: Stob nan Cabar of Buachaille Etive Beag from the north-east.

its more haughty sibling; begging noisily for attention and oozing charisma, offering a variety of interesting scrambling routes, and with a summit ridge that is nothing short of delightful. Indeed, from Glen Etive it is Buachaille Etive Beag, with its perfect triangular shape, which gets the better of its bigger relation. This walk and scramble takes in the best that the mountain has to offer.

Beside the busy A82, the lovely Lochan na Fola offers a classic view of Buachaille Etive Beag mirrored in its rush-dotted waters. The 'lochan of blood' takes its grisly name from an incident in 1543, when a rather irritated Cunningham of Glenure and sons charged and killed several Rannoch clansmen who had stolen their cattle, throwing the bodies into the water. A couple of hundred metres east of the lochan is a large car park. From it a signpost proclaiming 'Public Footpath Glen Etive 5' points south-west towards the perfectly parabolic Làirig Gartain, which separates Buachailles Etive Beag and Mòr.

Stob Dubh of Buachaille Etive Beag and the Stob Dubh above Glenceitlein from the River Etive below Coileitir.

Scramblers should follow this path for a kilometre before bearing across the moorland to the eastern corner of Stob nan Cabar. Be warned though: this is a scramble of 'character', and anyone with an aversion to vegetation, or expecting another Curved Ridge, will be disappointed. Aim for the right-hand corner of the obvious large crag, the base of which can be followed up rightwards until a weakness leads to more open ground. The slopes above are broken by many rock outcrops, but a way can be picked through them without undue difficulty. Though pleasingly airy, the situations never grow particularly exposed. Not far from the top, either make a rising traverse leftwards, or scramble up directly to the rocky knoll crowning what is now clearly not a true peak, but a truncated ridge.

From Stob nan Cabar, an initially level broad-backed ridge of rough knolls and lochan-filled hollows leads, over a kilometre or so, to the 925m (3019ft) summit of Stob Coire Raineach, the lower of Buachaille Etive Beag's two Munros. On a good day the going is very pleasant, but in cloud this gradually steepening ascent can seem interminable. Stob Coire Raineach can also be easily climbed by following the Làirig Gartain path for 3km and attacking the slopes of the shallow corrie south of the peak. The summit is a good one – a fine viewpoint for the Aonach Eagach in particular, but the prospect of Buachaille Etive Beag's other Munro, Stob Dubh, is most inviting.

The descent to the 750m bealach separating the two summits is short but brutal. A slightly more civilised rise leads onwards to a minor

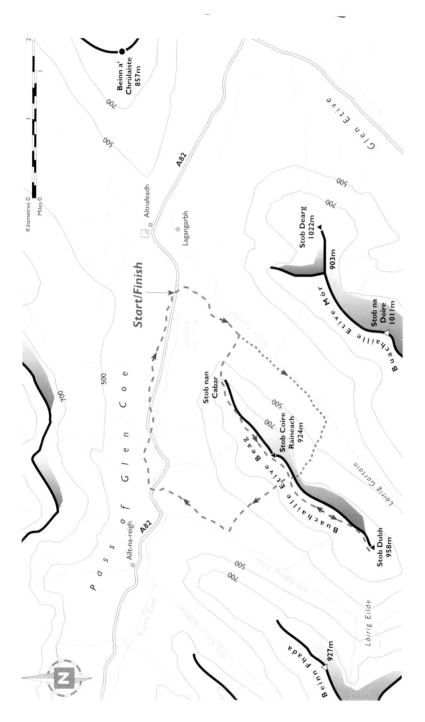

Beinn a'
Chrùlaiste
857m

700

500

A82

Altnafeadh

Lagangarbh

Glen Etive

500

700

Stob Dearg
1022m

903m

Buachaille Etive Mòr

Stob na
Doire
1011m

Start/Finish

River Coupall

Lairig Gartain

500

Stob nan
Cabar

500

700

Stob Coire
Raineach
924m

Buachaille Etive Beag

Stob Dubh
958m

500
700

700

P a s s   o f   G l e n   C o e

500

700

Allt-na-reigh

A82

River Coe

Allt Coire Gabhail

Allt Lairig Eilde

500
700

Lairig Eilde

Beinn Fhada

927m

Kilometres 0
Miles 0
2

high-point where the ridge levels, narrowing into a beautiful easy arête perched above the precipices of a small corrie to the north-west. The walking this provides is pure pleasure, easing the small remaining climb to the 958m (3129ft) summit of Stob Dubh. The high point appears on a short stony summit ridge poised airily between the sky and deep glens on either side – surprisingly, perhaps, in a better situation than anything similar on Buachaille Etive Mòr. The walk is not a long one, and lunch may be a good excuse to linger on this beautiful summit for a while, enjoying an eagle's view of Glen Etive. When the time comes to descend however, return along the arête to the bealach, then romp down the slopes to either the north-west or south-east. The descent north-west into the Làirig Èilde is more interesting, despite extra walking close to the main road at the walk's end. A path picked up just below the bealach descends to the right of the longest of the ravines cleaving the shallow corrie.

The descent is remorseless for 400m, following the ridge between two ravines until, near the Allt Làirig Èilde, the path traverses rightwards to join the Làirig Èilde footpath. The views up the starkly beautiful Làirig Èilde are dominated by the Sròn na Làirig: a steep and in places very narrow rocky spur which provides a fine scramble up Stob Coire Sgreamhach in the Bidean nam Bian massif. The path descends briskly to the road, opposite a huge cairn like a giant beehive.

Dating from the times of wolves, this 'coffin cairn' was located at the junction of routes over which coffins were borne from the surrounding glens for burial on Eilean Munde in Loch Leven. Such journeys were commonplace in the Highlands, and it became traditional to build a cairn at rest stops and for other travellers to add a stone and offer a prayer. It is easy to see how a large cairn would

develop in such a prominent place. The cairn was destroyed by navvies working on the 1785 Glen Coe road who fancied that money was buried in it, but restored by the National Trust for Scotland in 1992.

The best return to the starting point is by the old Glen Coe road, now a de luxe footpath. From the cairn, either ford the River Coe or follow the A82 towards Glen Coe until it crosses the river, then backtrack along the old road. The bridges over the numerous streams are still intact and, apart from one brief section, the old road can be followed all the way back to the car park at a pace much more conducive to scenic appreciation than is possible in a car.

Stob nan Cabar from Lochan na Fola.

BEINN A' CHRÙLAISTE AND MEALL BHALACH

Distance: 9.5km (6 miles).
Ascent: 695m (2280ft).
Start/finish: Kingshouse (GR260547), on loop road off A82 at the head of Glen Coe.
Maps: OS Landranger 41 *Ben Nevis, Fort William & surrounding area* or Outdoor Leisure 38 *Ben Nevis & Glencoe* or Pathfinder 306 *Central Rannoch Moor.* Harveys Walker's Map or Superwalker *Glen Coe* (covers Beinn a' Chrùlaiste only).
Terrain: Straightforward walking mostly on heath and turf.
Stalking information: Black Corries Estate, tel. 01855 851272 (September-February).

Gaelic names
 Beinn a' Chrùlaiste (bYn a **chroo**:lashtya): Rocky mountain.
 Meall Bhalach (myowl **va**:loch): Mound of the boy.
 Allt a' Bhalaich (owlt a **va**:lich): Stream of the boys.
 Meall nan Ruadhag (myowl nan **roo**aghak): Mound of the red
  roes.

In the company of so many higher and more eye-catching hills, Beinn a' Chrùlaiste and its even more pudding-shaped satellite Meall Bhalach might seem hardly worthy of a second glance, let alone the effort of climbing them. Dismissal on these grounds would be a great mistake, however, as the views of Buachaille Etive Mòr from Beinn a' Chrùlaiste are peerless. The panorama over Rannoch Moor too is one of the finest, giving a better impression of its sheer size and the great peaks which encircle it than is offered by the more distracting and less strategically positioned higher summits.

Top: Beinn a' Chrùlaiste and the Kingshouse.

The Kingshouse Hotel, where the walk starts, is already 245m above sea level, leaving only a 600m climb to the summit of Beinn a' Chrùlaiste over a distance of a just 3.5km. As a result this is a very easy walk, ideal for a relaxed morning or afternoon. Sunrise on Buachaille Etive Mòr from up here is a sight which should engrave itself on the memory. If a longer outing is sought, the twin humps of Meall Bhalach give pleasant walking and interesting views of the Blackwater Reservoir and down towards Kinlochleven.

Set in the western corner of Rannoch Moor and faced squarely by Buachaille Etive Mòr, the Kingshouse is one of the most spectacularly situated hotels in Scotland – and a fine starting and finishing point for a walk, with its historic climbers' bar. It is situated on the military road built between Stirling and Fort William, which has already been encountered in previous walks.

Beinn a' Chrùlaiste and Meall Bhalach above the Kingshouse.

The road was mostly constructed in the years after 1750 to aid the suppression of the Highlands following the battle of Culloden. A brutal regime was imposed in a very successful attempt to quell the Highlands by destroying its culture. This included shaming teaching of Gaelic, in favour of English, and the outlawing of the public playing of bagpipes and the wearing of the traditional tartan plaid, with dire punishments for miscreants. The plaid was not just a fundamental item of clothing: it also provided a warm, midge-proof bed and bivouac. Outlawing these would have been equivalent to towing away a modern traveller's caravan.

The section of the road between Loch Tulla and the Kingshouse, parts of which are now followed by the West Highland Way, was built with extraordinary speed under the direction of Major Caulfeild (successor to the better-known General Wade, who built the Highlands' first cross-country roads after the earlier 1715 Jacobite rising) in 1752. The Kingshouse, one of the country's oldest licensed inns and once a cattle drover's stance (overnight stop) and notorious haunt of smugglers, also dates from this period.

Beside it a stone arch bridge crosses the tea-coloured waters of the River Etive which drains this part of the moor, over which a single track road leads northwards, soon turning abruptly left. Here a stile and gate lead onto a track which disappears across the moor in the direction of the lonely Black Corries Lodge. About 200m along the track, just before a bridge, turn off northwards along the bank of

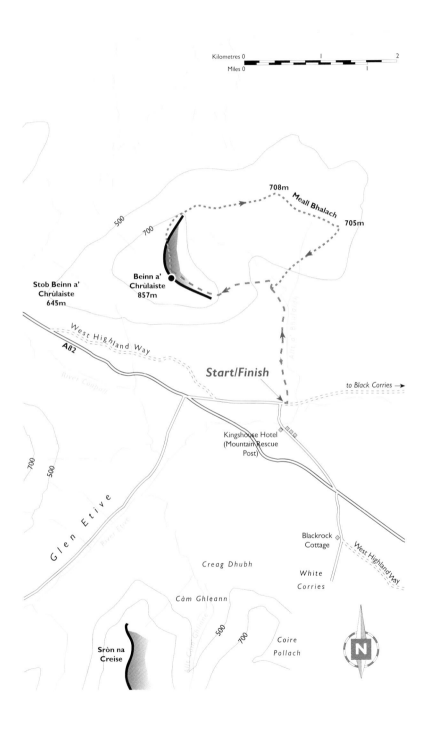

the Allt a' Bhalaich. A path, intermittent in places, climbs gradually up alongside the burn for about 1.5km, before traversing above a small slot-like rocky gorge.

As the stream starts to curl rightwards past the gorge, bear off up rough heathery slopes below Beinn a' Chrùlaiste's steepening eastern nose. This gives an uncompromising but rapid ascent, with views over Rannoch Moor which improve steadily. Before long they are simply stunning. The angle eases gradually as the nose merges with a domed summit plateau, crowned by a large cairn and a trig pillar encircled by a stone windbreak. The best viewpoint up here is not the summit, but amongst the rocks 200m or so to the south, where the ground begins to fall away. From here the Buachaille is quite a sight, and the perspectives of the Glen Coe and Blackmount peaks are rather good as well.

From the plateau a broad, turfy ridge curves north and then east towards Meall Bhalach, giving a pleasant and easy descent. Every year, thousands of cattle and sheep were driven over the pass between Meall Bhalach and Meall nan Ruadhag before the drover's stance at Ciaran disappeared below the surface of the Blackwater Reservoir, which now dominates the view to the north. Constructed between 1905 and 1909 to provide power to the aluminium works in Kinlochleven, the reservoir was was one of the last big schemes hand-engineered by the tough, itinerant navvies who had made Britain's canals and railways.

Their stark existence living and working on the site is vividly recounted in Patrick McGill's novel *Children of the Dead End*. Understandably partial to drink, many would brave the military road from Kinlochleven over the pass known as the Devil's Staircase to the Kingshouse in all weathers, resulting inevitably in tales of spring snows disgorging corpses still clutching whisky bottles. In recent years the level of the reservoir has fallen very low, revealing huge areas of bare bed. Drowned buildings were seen again in 1996.

Little effort is required to reach either of the twin stony tops of Meall a' Bhalach, from where the best descent is provided by the south-western slopes. Cross the Allt a' Bhalach below the gorge, and follow the path along its bank back towards the Kingshouse.

Looking west-south-west from Beinn a' Chrùlaiste across Rannoch Moor.

WALK 15

THE NORTHERN PEAKS
OF THE BLACKMOUNT

Distance: 14km (8.5 miles).
Ascent: 1160m (3800ft).
Start/Finish: The Kingshouse Hotel (GR259546), on loop road off the A82 at the head of Glen Coe.
Maps: OS Landrangers 41 *Ben Nevis, Fort William & surrounding area* and 50 *Glen Orchy & surrounding area* or Outdoor Leisure 38 *Ben Nevis & Glencoe* or Pathfinders 306 *Central Rannoch Moor* and 320 *Loch Tulla*. Harveys Walker's Map or Superwalker *Glen Coe*.
Terrain: Open moorland followed by sustained medium grade scrambling in spectacular surroundings – loose in its lower section, but up beautiful clean slabby rock higher up – then generally straightforward walking over high and spacious stony ridges.
Stalking Information: Blackmount Estate, tel. 01838 400225/400269 (September-late October).

Gaelic names

Sròn na Creise (strawn na **kraysh**): Nose of Creise (see below).

Stob a' Ghlais Choire (stob a' **ghlash** chora): Peak of the grey-green corrie.

Creag Dhubh (krayk **ghoo**): Black crag.

Creise (kraysh): Origin obscure.

Mam Coire Easain (maam kora **es**Yn): Breast of the corrie of the little waterfalls.

Clach Leathad (klach **lay**at): Stone of the (broad) slope.

Meall a' Bhuiridh (myowl a **voo**:ree): Mound of the roaring.

Càm Ghleann (ka:m ghlyown): Crooked glen.

Lochan na H-Achlaise (lochan na **hachla**: sha): lochan of the armpit.

Allt Càm Ghlinne (owlt ka:m **ghlee**nya): stream of the crooked glen.

Top: Sròn na Creise and Beinn Mhic Chasgaig from the River Coupall.

The southern edge of Rannoch Moor's western arm is defined by group of a fine peaks constituting the northern half of the massif which has become popularly known as the Blackmount. Seen from the east on the A82 above the islet-studded waters of Lochan na h-Achlaise, they have a beautiful stark simplicity of form which has made this one of the most photographed views in the Highlands. Like views of Buachaille Etive Mòr's Stob Dearg, hardly a year seems to go by without it appearing in a calendar somewhere.

The northern Blackmount peaks are equally impressive from the Kingshouse, and although the comparatively gentle northern slopes of Meall a' Bhuiridh have become increasingly taken over by the skiing industry, the craggy sweep of Stob a' Ghlais Choire and the steep rocky nose of Sròn na Creise are almost as imposing as neighbouring Stob Dearg. Sròn na Creise is a truly magnificent scramble, without which no traverse of these hills would be complete.

Scrambling on Sròn na Creise, with Stob Dearg in the background.

The Kingshouse bar provides a very agreeable start and finish point. Take the hotel's southern access road, cross the A82, and negotiate rough open moorland below the spur of Creag Dhubh, aiming for the broken buttress falling north-eastwards from the tip of Sròn na Creise. It is worthwhile contouring a little up into the Càm Ghleann, as here the Allt Càm Ghlinne tumbles over beautiful polished pink and grey boulders, providing a superb foreground for Buachaille Etive Mòr and an easier crossing than lower down in times of spate.

So many enjoyable lines can be taken at a reasonable level of difficulty on Sròn na Creise that describing any specific route is probably unnecessary, and might even spoil the fun. Initially, however, two obvious choices present themselves. One is the broken ground left of the obvious reddish gully which divides the nose. This is very loose, with lots of scree and unstable rubble which requires care, but eventually steepens into a buttress of superb rough slabs, with the gully tapering down into the moors below. This buttress can also be approached up the gully itself: also quite loose, but the worst can be avoided by more solid grassy ground to the right. A huge boulder perched on a grassy shoulder on the right provides a good spot for some late breakfast, before crossing the gully's red scree to the base of the buttress proper, where the true scrambling starts.

The situations are superb. The views of Buachaille Etive Mòr are remarkable and only improve with height, as does the panorama of the Mamores and Ben Nevis. A line can be picked which is nowhere very hard, but the scrambling is airy, sustained, and totally engrossing – and there are plenty of harder variations to be enjoyed by those so inclined.

All good things must end, however, and eventually the buttress runs out onto a broad shoulder which leads up steadily to the 996m

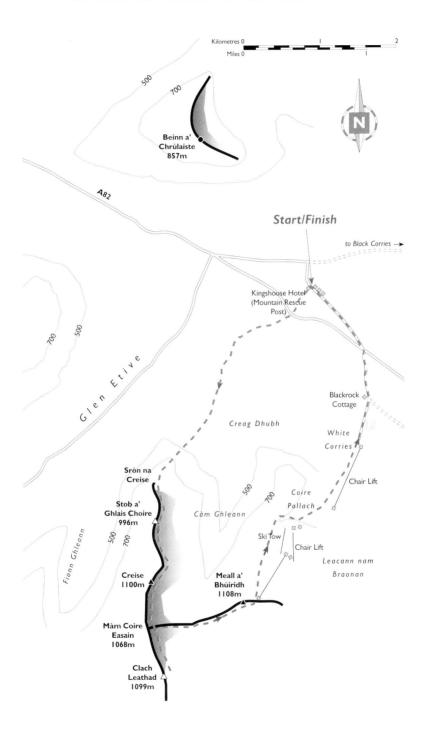

Kilometres 0   1   2
Miles 0   1

500
700

**Beinn a'
Chrùlaiste
857m**

A82

N

Start/Finish

to Black Corries →

Kingshouse Hotel
(Mountain Rescue
Post)

G l e n   E t i v e

700   *500*

Blackrock
Cottage

Creag Dhubh

*White
Corries*

Chair Lift

**Sròn na
Creise**

*Coire
Pollach*

Càm Ghleann

500   *700*

**Stob a'
Ghlais Choire
996m**

Ski Tow

Chair Lift

Fionn Ghleann

500   *700*

*Leacann nam
Braonan*

**Creise
1100m**

**Meall a'
Bhùiridh
1108m**

**Màm Coire
Easain
1068m**

**Clach
Leathad
1099m**

Creag Dhubh, Meall a' Bhuiridh, Creise, Stob a' Ghlais Choire and Sròn na Creise from the Kingshouse.

(3268ft) Top of Stob a' Ghlais Coire. This offers interesting wild views to the west, although elsewhere they are surprisingly not as good as from the ascent of Sròn na Creise itself.

Descending southwards from the summit an intriguing pinnacle is passed, high above the open corrie of the Càm Ghleann. The 1100m (3608ft) Munro of Creise is just an easy rise away, giving good views of Meall a' Bhuiridh, the walk's final summit, which from here is an austere reddish pyramid of almost anthropogenic regularity. The next Top, Màm Coire Easain (1068m, 3506ft), is reached by a gentle stroll along the edge of a broken east-facing eascarpment.

Slightly beyond the cairn is a narrowish rocky rib which will soon provide the descent to the base of Meall a' Bhuiridh's clean-cut western ridge. First, however, the described walk detours a mere kilometre to the south off OS Landranger map 41 onto map 50. It is worth buying another map for this excursion if necessary, as the crag-rimmed shoulder of 1098m (3602ft) Clach Leathad does give fine views towards Stob Ghabhar and the crescent of peaks above Bridge of Orchy to the south-east. No single viewpoint or visit is remotely sufficient for a full impression to be gained of Rannoch Moor, but Clach Leathad provides another fine piece of the overall picture.

Having returned to just before the cairn of Màm Coire Easain, descend the previously mentioned steep but perfectly straightforward rib to the bealach between the Càm Ghleann and Coire Easain, which is decorated with a jewel-like lochan. Above the bealach, a lengthy haul up an increasingly rocky and well-defined ridge leads to the fine 1108m (3636ft) summit of Meall a' Bhuiridh, set on a shattered rocky ridge which slopes craggily towards Rannoch Moor.

Just 150m east of the summit is the top station of one of the White Corries ski-tows. The best way to avoid most of the parephernalia of the ski-slopes is to follow the broad ridge which descends northwards towards Creag Dhubh, dropping eastwards into the elevated basin of Coire Pollach, where beauty still survives in the meanderings of the Allt nan Giubhas through upland meadows. In poor weather, however, the ski-tows provide a useful guide into the corrie.

Once past the buildings of Coire Pollach, drop directly to the White Corries car-park by a path which descends close to the line of the chairlift. From the car-park, follow the road past Blackrock Cottage (owned by the Ladies Scottish Climbing Club), cross the A82 and return directly to the Kingshouse, where cool liquid refreshment can be enjoyed even as boots are removed.

WALK 16

THE SOUTHERN
BLACKMOUNT PEAKS

Distance: 18km (11 miles).
Ascent: 1230m (4050ft).
Start/Finish: Victoria Bridge public car park (GR271419), reached by turning off A82 at Bridge of Orchy onto A8005 for 5km.
Maps: OS Landranger 50 *Glen Orchy & surrounding area* or Outdoor Leisure 38 *Ben Nevis & Glencoe* or Pathfinder 320 *Loch Tulla*. Harveys Walker's Map or Superwalker *Glen Coe*.
Terrain: Some quite rough ground, with a brief section of generally straightforward scrambling on the Aonach Eagach of Stob Ghabhar. Great attention should be paid to navigation in poor visibility.
Stalking Information: A noticeboard at Victoria Bridge public car park gives daily information on stalking activity in the Blackmount Estate, including preferred routes for walkers. Tel. 01838 400225/400269 (September-late October).

Gaelic names

> **Stob Ghabhar** (stob **ghow**ar): Goat peak.
> **Aonach Eagach** (oe:noch **e**goch): Notched ridge.
> **Stob a' Choire Odhair** (stob a chor **aw**ar): Peak of the dun-coloured corrie.
> **Coire na Muic** (kora na **mooee**chk): Corrie of the pig.
> **Allt/Coire Toaig** (owlt/kora **taw**eek): Possibly from *taoig* (**too**-eek), meaning a fit of passion.
> **Coirein Lochain** (koryin **loch**Yn`): Corrie of the little loch.
> **Sròn nan Giubhas** (strawn nan **gyoo**as): Nose of the Scots pines.
> **Sròn a' Ghearrain** (strawn a **ya**ran): Nose of the gelding.
> **Abhainn Shira:** from abhainn siòrabh (avYn **shyoa**:ra): lasting river.

Top: Stob Ghabhar from near Auch to the south-east.

Looking towards Ben Cruachan from the summit of Stob Ghabhar.

Stob Ghabhar is a very fine peak, home to some of the wildest corrie and glen scenery covered by this book, while being very accessible from the roadhead at Victoria Bridge. It also sports a comparatively little known rocky arête called - and here's a surprise - the Aonach Eagach. Though not in the same league as its more famous namesake above Glen Coe in terms of length or difficulty, it still provides an entertaining brief scramble of great quality.

Neighbouring Stob Ghabhar, and a logical addition to its traverse, is Stob a' Choire Odhair. The true steepness of this lower Munro, which appears quite gentle from some angles, is revealed in the classic view of the Blackmount range from the vicinity of Loch Bà, where its striking simplicity of form provides the perfect foil for Stob Ghabhar's complex array of ridge, buttress and corrie. The walk described provides an interesting and varied exploration of the two peaks.

With its saucer-shaped Coire na Muic, Stob Ghabhar is quite a well-formed peak seen from the large public car park near Victoria Bridge, but hides its best features from here. A path skirts the back of a stand of trees, joining the road to Forest Lodge just before the

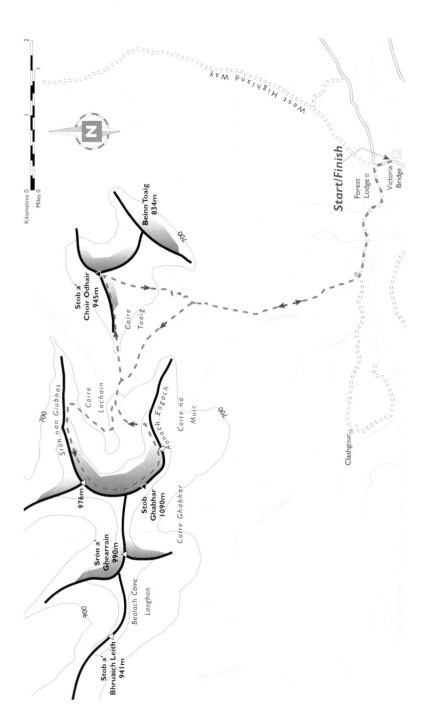

bridge itself – another on the old military road. Forest Lodge nestles in another, larger stand of trees. Before it, a track bears off westwards towards the farm of Clashgour.

Take this track for 1.5km along the banks of the lovely Abhainn Shira to a distinctly odd little corrugated iron hut. It may come as a surprise that this was the Clashgour schoolhouse, which, perhaps even more surprisingly, is now a hut for the relatively large Glasgow University Mountaineering Club. The views from its vicinity are marred by forestry, but still retain much of their former glory: out over the great wide basin of the headwaters of the Abhainn Shira and the River Kinglass, above which the Loch Etive hills raise a barrier of wild, unkempt flanks.

Just past the hut, a stalkers' path turns off north through a broad gap in the plantations fringing the river, following the east bank of the Allt Toaig. This climbs very pleasantly up the lazy Coire Toaig below the flank of Stob a' Choire Odhair and its stunted twin, Beinn Toaig. After 2.5km a path branches off rightwards, zigzagging up the SSW spur of Stob a' Choire Odhair. This will provide the best way down at the end of the walk.

Looking West from the Abhainn Shira near the turn-off up Coire Toaig.

Towards the head of the corrie the path fades, but just about makes it onto the broad and knobbly bealach separating the two Munros of the walk, from which Stob a' Choire Odhair appears as a bulky pyramid. From the bealach, contour into the hanging glacial hollow of Coirein Lochain. It is well worth detouring slightly to the beautiful lochan which occupies this impressive glacial amphitheatre. Some 400m above loom the crags of Stob Ghabhar, its twin summit buttresses split by the Upper Couloir – a classic winter climb which first succumbed in 1897, to a party led by A.E. Mayland, after many frustrated attempts.

The suggested itinerary of this walk might seem odd at first, but means that sunlight should still be flooding the corrie on arrival at the lochan. The best line out of Coirein Lochain onto Sròn nan Giubhas is also far simpler to locate from below than in descent. Contour round to below the eastern nose of Sròn nan Giubhas, where a way can be found up a short corridor of steep but reasonable ground onto its knolly crest at around 780m.

The nose gains height pleasantly, with fine views into Coirein Lochain, steepening before merging with a gently sloping granite

plateau. Follow the corrie rim around to a cairn crowning the 974m (3197ft) high-point of Sròn nan Giubhas. Onwards from this Top, a miniscule dip leads to the summit slopes of Stob Ghabhar, where a change from pink and grey granite boulders to more grassy terrain marks a transition to a band of beautifully textured metamorphic gneiss.

The 1087m (3565ft) summit cairn is reached without much extra effort. From here many of the surrounding peaks are not as impressive as from some other viewpoints, being seen largely side-on to the grain of the land, but the scene has a wonderful wild grandeur to it; especially south-west towards Ben Cruachan, north over the Blackmount's tangle of ridges, and north-east over Rannoch Moor. Close by, rusting boundary posts march eastwards from Stob Ghabhar's western Top, Sròn a' Ghearrain, which is worth a visit for the energetic.

Now comes the best part of the day. A descent is made close to the line of the boundary posts until they bear off down a broad shoulder to the south-east, which provides a useful escape for non-scramblers. This would be a shame, however, because the ridge which continues eastwards soon narrows into the entertaining rocky switchback of the Aonach Eagach. One narrow notch on this ridge might give pause for thought, but the scrambling is never hard.

East of the Aonach Eagach's 991m high point marks the end of difficulties, and as the now far broader ridge begins to curve south-east, begin looking for the descent northwards back to the bealach below Stob a' Choire Odhair. Take care if the visibility is poor. A clear path down rough slopes with a fair amount of scree leads steeply back to the bealach, after which 1km of walking over and between rocky knolls gains the base of Stob a' Choire Odhair's broad and rocky west ridge. A fairly stiff clamber of 230m lands you on the stony summit dome.

As a viewpoint for Rannoch Moor, Stob a' Choire Odhair rivals Beinn a' Chrùlaiste (Walk 14). It is also a fine platform for surveying the features of Stob Ghabhar, which from here is more regally graceful than spectacular. On a warm summer's afternoon, its cairn is a place to relax and just soak up the scenery. When you do leave, bear SSW from the summit down initially rocky gentle slopes. As these steepen after a little more than 500m, a path should be picked up, descending swiftly back to the Coire Toaig path, and the track to Victoria Bridge.

WALK 17
ACROSS RANNOCH MOOR

Distance: 32km (20 miles).
Ascent: 240m (800ft).
Start: Rannoch Station (GR423578), reached by train from Bridge of Orchy, where there is a car park at the station.
Finish: Bridge of Orchy (GR297396).
Maps: OS Landrangers 41 *Ben Nevis, Fort William & surrounding area* and 42 *Glen Garry & Loch Rannoch area* and 50 *Glen Orchy & surrounding area* or Pathfinders 307 *Loch Rannoch (west)* and 306 *Central Rannoch Moor* and 320 *Loch Tulla*.
Terrain: Easy walking on tracks, then paths which can be boggy. The mid-section of the walk is over rough and often wet trackless ground with heavily peat-hagged areas. In poor visibility this requires proficiency in map and ground-reading, though loch shores (generally firm, dry ground) aid navigation. The final leg of the walk follows the West Highland Way, and then a quiet single track road.
Stalking Information: Rannoch Deer Management Association, tel. 01882 633248 (September-February) and Blackmount Estate, tel. 01838 400225/400269 (September-late October).

Gaelic names
> **Beinn a' Chreachain** (bYn a **chrech**Yn˙): Mountain of the bare summit.
> **Beinn Achaladair** (bYn **acha**latar): Mountain of the farm by the hard water.
> **Dubh Lochan** (**doo** lochan): Dark small loch.
> **Loch Laidon:** Origin obscure.
> **Loch Tulla** (loch **too**la): loch of the mound or knoll.
> **Stob na Cruaiche** (stob na **kroo**eecha): Peak of the heaps (probably referring to peat stacks).
> **Tigh na Cruaiche** (tY na **kroo**eecha): House of the heaps.
> **Coire Bà** (kora **bà**:): Corrie of the cows.
> **Eilean Molach** (elyan **mo**-loch): Rough/hairy island.
> **Mam Carraigh** (ma:m **ca**-ree). Breast of the pillar.
> **Doire Darach** (dora **da**roch): Oak wood.

Top: Looking towards the Bridge of Orchy peaks from the end of the track through the plantations above Loch Laidon.

Rannoch Moor, which covers 300 square miles (770 sq km), has traditionally suffered a lurid reputation as a wilderness of bottomless mud which eats people. Hopefully this impression is fading. Though certainly demanding respect, it is in fact a colourful, complex mosaic of environments, including glacier-smoothed hills and basins, bogs, heaths, streams and lochans, lochs and islands.

Nor is it a true wilderness, and those expecting such may be disappointed. Its very bareness and wetness is a result of the burning and felling of the forest which once blanketed it entirely, and whose skeletal stumps now pepper its innumerable hags of eroding peat. Derelict traces of human settlement are scattered across it. Roads, railways and tracks criss-cross it, and large areas have been planted with fenced ranks of conifers, entailing artificial drainage on a huge scale.

Mountain devotees might dismiss this walk – but I hope curiosity will triumph, for unexpected delights await those who throw preconceptions to the wind. Crossing that vast open space watching the slow change of the encircling mountain ranges is an experience which should, on days either of huge blue skies or clouds pressed darkly overhead, leave images that linger long in the spaces of the mind.

This is a walk best enjoyed during a dry spell. Judicious use of a vehicle and bicycles will help: a bike left at Victoria Bridge for the final 5.5km of the return to the starting point at Bridge of Orchy may be appreciated at the end of quite a long day. A half-hour train journey is necessary to reach Rannoch Station: a fine start to the walk, lending proceedings an expeditionary flavour. The charming Victorian station at Bridge of Orchy is 300 metres up the road opposite the hotel.

The train traverses ever-changing scenery on the south side of the moor: the gnarled pines of Crannach Wood – a remnant of the once great forest of Caledon beneath the ramparts and corries of Beinn a' Chreachain and Beinn Achaladair; the less varied woodlands of the Rannoch Forest plantations, where in places the track had to be 'floated' on brushwood to prevent it sinking; and finally open moor to the isolated and peaceful Rannoch Station. On the platform here is a post office, and a summer tea-shop serving delicious home baking. A footbridge crosses the railway to the station car park, from where a track turning right past a small white cottage doubles back over the railway line towards the Dubh Lochan and Loch Laidon.

Despite heading towards the coast, this walk goes mostly against the drainage of Rannoch Moor. The Moor was a centre for ice-cap development: something clearly demonstrated in the final 1000-year spasm of the last ice-age – the Loch Lomond Advance, which ended 10,000 years ago. After a brief ice-free spell the moor once

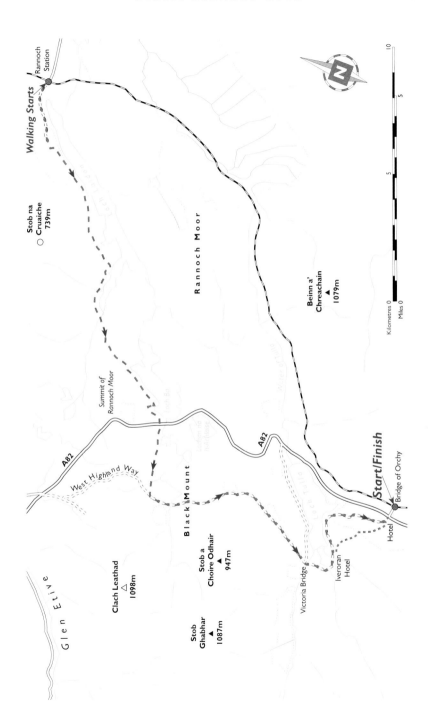

more filled with ice sufficiently thick to reduce surrounding peaks to isolated ridges dividing long glaciers which flowed outwards from this central high basin like the spokes of a wheel.

This is reflected in today's drainage: the moor itself is the watershed in this part of the highlands, draining northwards by Loch Treig and the River Spean; north-west by the Leven; to the south-west by the Etive; southwards from Loch Tulla by the Orchy; and all the way to the east coast and the Tay by the Tummel. Today it is not too hard to imagine Buachaille Etive Mòr as an island of rhyolite splitting the two mighty outflow glaciers which shaped the brooding trenches of Glen Etive and Glen Coe.

The track passes a gate to the birch and willow-softened plantation which hugs Loch Laidon's north shore; a sign proclaims that you are following the footpath to Glencoe. Beyond estate cottages and the sandy isthmus separating the Dubh Lochan from the larger Loch Laidon, the track forks. Unless planning to hug the birch-fringed loch shore (scenic, but time-consuming), take the right-hand fork – again signposted 'footpath to Glencoe' – into the plantation. Electricity lines intrude briefly until the path rises above them into the dense trees. Clearings offer views of the peaks earlier skirted by the train.

Around 2km after forking, the track drops to a turning platform for forestry vehicles, and another 'footpath to Glencoe' sign at a superb viewpoint points down towards the loch. Following a short, sharp descent the path shadows the electricity lines once more, but it soon becomes possible to ignore them. After 1.5km or so, a gate and stile cross the deer fence of the plantation's edge.

Loch Laidon and Rannoch Moor skyscape from Tigh na Cruaiche.

The Blackmount peaks, Buachaille Etive Mòr and Beinn a' Chrùlaiste from Loch Laidon, Rannoch Moor.

Here, the path forks. Take the lower left-hand fork, which meanders towards the loch before rising again to give good views back towards Rannoch. The path curves slowly west around the slopes of Stob na Cruaiche, and a magnificent panorama of the peaks south of the moor opens up. The path branches again, the left-hand branch slanting below the electricity lines to the ruins of Tigh na Cruaiche, part of which is roofed.

This is a good place for a rest, and perhaps some early lunch. On a fine day Loch Laidon is ethereally beautiful, seemingly torn from a piece of the sky. Safe from deer, islands in this and neighbouring Loch Bà are bursting with woodland, giving some impression of what most of Scotland would be like if deer numbers were maintained at levels which allowed seedlings to grow.

Their population was once partly controlled by wolves, but since the last wolf was shot in the 18th century, they have multiplied to the point where they are the most important single shaping factor of the Highland landscape. Their hunting provides income for many Highland estates, who are under strong economic pressure to sustain unnaturally high population densities because estate value traditionally relates to herd size.

From Tigh na Cruaiche, cross the stream and follow muted vehicle tracks to a coil gate in an electric fence. This is a cattle enclosure, and black, brown and cream specimens may be seen snoozing on the drier mounds while you strike across often wet moor in the direction of the Blackmount. After roughly 1.5km the opposite side of the enclosure is reached: exit by another coil-gate in the south-east corner. Past the fence is an area of quaking bog, where it is possible to produce standing ripples in the surface vegetation by jumping up and down. Jewelled dragonflies swarm here in late summer.

It is best to aim for Loch Laidon roughly halfway along its western arm: a maze of gorgeous sandbars and beaches, rocky bays, hagged creeks, and sheltered lilypad-studded waters reflecting a huge sky. Skinny-dipping country par excellence, but beware of unexpected fishing dinghies! Those who bring binoculars may be rewarded with an otter or a spectacular great northern or red-throated diver. Tramp to the tip of the loch's arm through a maze of glacial till hummocks. Tussocky ground gives hard going, slightly ameliorated by deer tracks, until the inflow stream can be crossed by boulder-hopping.

Now walk across the moor in a south-westerly direction, aiming for the northerly arm of Loch Bà. There are plenty of peat hags on this section, forcing tiring detours. Do not be tempted to cross hags which are clearly soft as some (especially those covered by lime-green Spaghnum moss) are potentially dangerous. In the unlikely (and avoidable) event of trouble, get a large surface area in contact with the bog, work any stuck limbs free, and squirm to solidity.

After a barely perceptible rise, glittering Loch Bà bursts into view, with the woods of the aptly named Eilean Molach directly ahead. A reasonably distinct path should be encountered running towards the main body of the loch, finding the best way along its crinkled shore to a green corrugated boatshed and the A82.

Any whom the walk has already satisfied may be tempted to hitch a lift back to Bridge of Orchy (vehicle owners wanting a shorter walk could leave bikes here). Otherwise a path ten metres north on the opposite side of the road gives pleasant tramping across the moor, with widening views across the enormous Coire Bà – in volume, the biggest corrie in Scotland – and the peaks of the Blackmount. Near the ruin of Bà Cottage, another old cattle stance, the path joins the West Highland Way. For 2.5km this follows the old military road between Loch Tulla and Fort William, before descending gently to the woods of Victoria Bridge: straightforward strolling through magnificent scenery, and a wonderfully relaxed end to the day.

If no bikes have been left here, the tramp back to Bridge of Orchy in the golden light of a Highland evening - broken perhaps by refreshment at the Inveroran Hotel - is still very pleasant. Passing through the delightful Caledonian forest remnant of the Doire Darach, the road is actually, in my view, a nicer walk than the West Highland Way over Màm Carraigh, which it joins again by the old bridge over the River Orchy for a final brief climb to the Bridge of Orchy Hotel.

WALK 18

BEN STARAV AND ITS SATELLITES

Distance: 17km (10.5 miles).
Ascent: 1700m (5600ft).
Start/finish: Junction of Glen Etive road with track to Coileitir (GR137468). There are numerous parking spaces along the verge.
Maps: OS Landranger 50 *Glen Orchy & surrounding area* or Pathfinder 319 *Head of Loch Etive.* Harveys Walker's Map or Superwalker *Glen Coe.*
Terrain: A steep initial ascent followed by mainly straightforward ridge-walking, with steadily increasing interest until Ben Starav, where easy scrambling is encountered. Finding the correct descent from Stob Coir' an Albannaich requires care in poor visibility.
Stalking Information: Glen Etive Estate, tel. 01855 851277. The longer option enters Dalness Estate, tel, 01855 851252.

Gaelic names

Ben Starav: Derivation uncertain: possibly from starbhanach (**star**vanach), meaning a stocky man, or from *starabhan* (**star**avan), meaning a rustling noise.

Allt Mheuran (owlt **vair**an): Pronged or branched stream.

Stob Coir' an Albannaich (stob kor an **al**apaneech): Peak of the corrie of the Scotsman.

Meall nan Eun (myowl nan **ee**-an): Mound of the birds.

Glas Bheinn Mhòr (glas vŸn **voa:r**): Big green/grey mountain.

Meall nan Trì Tighearnan (myowl nan tree **tyee**-arnan): Mound of the three lords.

Beinn nan Aighenan (bŸn nan **Y**anan): Mountain of the hind.

Allt nam Meirleach (owlt nam **mayr**loch): Stream of the thieves.

Stob Coire Dhèirg (stob kora **ye**rak): Peak of the red corrie.

Coire an Fhir-Lèith (kora an ir **lay**): Corrie of the grey man.

Glen Etive: From *Eite* (**ay**tcha), a troublesome sprite of Celtic myth which inhabited Loch Etive.

Beinn Chaorach (bŸn **choe**:roch): sheep mountain.

Top: Bidean nam Bian, Buachaille Etive Beag and Stob Dubh from the north ridge of Ben Starav.

Rising in one great sweep to 1078m (3541ft) straight out of the salt waters of Loch Etive, Ben Starav is one of the grandest mountains of the western seaboard, and the highest British peak to stand with its toes in the sea. With fine ridges enclosing a beautifully sculpted north-eastern corrie, it presides regally over its lower subjects, dominating any view down the lower half of Glen Etive.

While less statuesque, its satellite Munros are also of great interest, with wild and bare elevated ridges offering delightful walking. The basic circuit described makes the best of this group in a day which is not too long, yet provides continually absorbing views and steadily increasing interest until a scrambly finale up to Ben Starav. For those seeking greater challenge, two longer options are also suggested.

The starting point is the turn-off to the cottage of Coileitir from the road down Glen Etive. A narrow track leads down to the River Etive which is crossed by a strangely urban bridge (reconstructed in 1992 by army engineers), high above huge dark pools between steep wooded banks. Remarkably, this bridge is below the river's highest recorded flood level in 1906 – a rise of a good 7m.

The track, which sends a branch up the glen to Glenceitlin, ends at the whitewashed cottage of Coileitir in the shelter of a grand horse chestnut tree. About 200m along the path to the south-west, another path branches off leftwards over very boggy ground, briefly shadowing a deer fence which it crosses by a stile that is the focus of a large quagmire. It climbs the hillside through bracken, crossing a stream to more marshy ground and finally sparse birch woodland to reach a stile on the opposite fence of the enclosure. Like most Highland woods, these fragments above Coileitir were dwindling under the onslaught of inflated numbers of hungry red deer, and while far from an ideal solution, the unsightly fences should at least prevent their extinction.

The path rises beside the fence for a short distance, then bears rightwards towards the Scots pine-encrusted gorge of the Allt Mheuran (worth a closer look). After a couple of hundred metres, attack the daunting grassy hillside above. The climb is remorseless, but on the positive side height is gained quickly, with splendid views of the golden bars of sediment dumped by the River Etive into the sudden stillness of Loch Etive, and the bright expanse of the famous slabs high on Beinn Trilleachan (a very popular spot for rock-climbers – at least when there's a breeze to keep the notorious midges tolerable). The lochan-spattered shoulder of Beinn Chaorach arrives without undue difficulty, from where the edge of rough Coire Glas is followed until vast boulder-peppered slopes, enlivened by excellent views of Ben Starav, lead to the short, pleasant summit ridge of Stob Coir' an Albannaich.

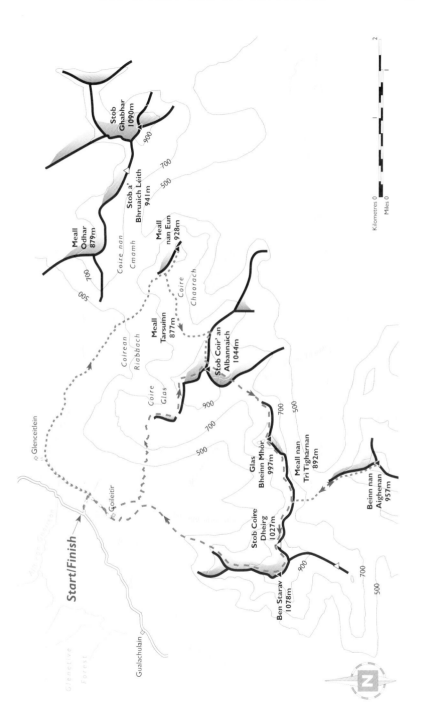

Stob Ghabhar 1090m

Stob a' Bhruaich Leith 941m

Meall Odhar 879m

Coire nan Cmamh

Meall nan Eun 928m

Coire Chaorach

Meall Tarsuinn 877m

Stob Coir' an Albannaich 1044m

Coirean Riabhach

Coire Glas

Glenceitlein

Coileitir

Glas Bheinn Mhòr 997m

Meall nan Tri Tigharnan 892m

Beinn nan Aighenan 957m

Stob Coire Dheirg 1027m

Start/Finish

Ben Starav 1078m

Gualachulain

Glenetive Forest

Kilometres 0

Miles 0

The 1044m (3425ft) summit gives perspectives of a lazy northern corrie, and an interesting but undistinguished panorama to the west. Stob Coir' an Albannaich is the younger brother of Ben Starav who ate too many chips: similar, but flabbier and less well formed. Its name, 'Peak of the corrie of the Scotsman', might seem odd until it is remembered that Scots were Christian immigrants from Ireland who eventually gave their name to a land previously dominated by the druidistic Picts.

An alternative approach for those seeking a longer day is up the delightful Glen Ceitlein (whose hillslopes in autumn are a virtually fluorescent orange), and over the Munro of Meall nan Eun – not an outstanding hill in its own right, but offering unusual dry-weather scrambling up bare granite stream beds from Coirean Riabhach. In poor visibility, however, take care locating Stob Coir' an Albannaich's east ridge from Meall Tarsuinn: the terrain is far from straightforward. This option adds 5km distance and 270m ascent.

The descent from Stob Coir' an Albannaich also requires care on a dreich day, as the featureless slopes south of the well defined summit ridge do not make the line of descent obvious, although a path is beginning to appear. A vague bulge in the steep bouldery slopes facing Glas Bheinn Mhòr – the next summit of the walk – marks the way down: don't be lured onto the obvious ridge of Sròn nan Cabar. From the bealach below, Glas Bheinn Mhòr presents a steep ridge of rocky outcrops, which levels into a fine airy promenade before steepening again below the mossy platform of the Munro's 997m (3258ft) summit.

Ben Starav from Meall nan Trì Tighearnan.

Stob Coir' an Albannaich from this angle looks suspiciously like something from the Cairngorms dumped on the western seaboard. Ben Starav is quite imposing from here, and remains so traversing the bump of Meall nan Trì Tighearnan, though its south-east face is too featureless to sustain the regal air the mountain projects northwards. The path climbing the sharp crest to the Top of Stob Coire Dhèirg promises entertainment, but unless legs are failing, its ascent should be postponed. Beinn nan Aighenan to the south is a worthy detour.

Wild and remote, and a lot of effort to reach if climbed on its own, it adds 4km and 490m ascent to the basic round. From the bealach below Stob Coire Dhèirg, slant down across the rough slopes of Meall nan Trì Tighearnan past several tiny lochans to a broad bealach at 618m, above which Beinn Aighenan's north ridge climbs craggily to a summit which offers wonderfully wild and unkempt views, particularly eastwards towards Loch Tulla. The return is by the same route.

Anyone who has had enough could now descend easily by the path which follows the Allt nam Meirleach – but that would be a pity, as the best is yet to come. Stob Coire Dhèirg's eastern ridge provides a remorseless ascent of 250m with fascinating rock scenery on the right, including a ridge of shattered granite which looks more Alpine than Scottish.

The rocky summit gives exciting prospects of the rest of Ben Starav across Coire an Fhir-Lèith, and of the approaching arête, which provides delectably easy scrambling (mostly avoidable on the south side) along a spine like a tumbledown dry-stone dyke. A final rise gains a stony and surprisingly flat plateau, which is followed westwards round the corrie rim and up to a fine summit, slightly north of which is a triangulation pillar.

Ben Starav makes its full height felt, and the views are well worth all the effort. Doing the circuit in this direction means that late afternoon or evening sunlight should shine off the waters of Loch Etive, lending the peaks that rich, almost translucent glow which only the western Highlands seem to manage. Fifty metres north of the cairn is a vertiginous perspective of the loch, and the slabs on Beinn Trilleachan. Mite-sized climbers on them, visible with binoculars, often give some idea of their scale.

The north ridge offers a fitting, if knee-testing, way down, and splendid views of Glas Bheinn Mhòr. Below its steep upper arête it broadens, thrusting almost directly towards Coileitir and the walk's end. From its base a path descends by the exuberant Allt nam Meirleach, which is peppered with irresistibly clear pools, then boggily to a bridge. More bog leads via the bank of the River Etive to the Coileitir track, and the end of a superb walk.

BEINN TRILLEACHAN

Distance: 11km (7 miles).
Ascent: 910m (2990ft).
Start/finish: Car park by ruined roadhead jetty (GR107449) at the end of the road down Glen Etive.
Maps: OS Landranger 50 *Glen Orchy & surrounding area* or Pathfinder 319 *Head of Loch Etive.*
Terrain: Mainly easy walking on broad, bare ridges, with one straightforward scrambly descent. Featureless ground around and to the south of the summit requires careful navigation in poor visibility.
Stalking Information: Forest Enterprise, tel. 01631 566155.

Gaelic names
> **Beinn Trilleachan** (bYn **treely**ochan): Mountain of sandpipers or oystercatchers.
> **Meall nan Gobhar** (myowl nan **gow**ar): Mound of the goat.
> **Aird Trilleachan** (aarhd **tree**lyochan): Point of sandpipers or oystercatchers.

Although dwarfed by Ben Starav, the rocky Corbett of Beinn Trilleachan is as much part of the defining nature of upper Loch Etive as its higher neighbour. In fact, its hillside above the loch is even rougher and steeper, at its steepest forming the 200m cream-coloured granite sweep of the Trilleachan Slabs. Beinn Trilleachan has been likened to an upturned boat - which is a polite way of saying it's a bit of a lump next to Ben Starav, but even so its ascent offers some highly unusual walking of great interest, and unmatched bird's-eye views of one of Scotland's most spectacular sea-lochs.

The best place to start is the car-park by the rapidly decaying jetty at the very end of the Glen Etive road just along the shore from the loch head, where there is space for about a dozen cars (further parking can be found a short way back up the road). This will save a little tarmac-

Top: Beinn Trilleachan from Aird Trilleachan, Loch Etive.
Left: Ben Starav and Glas Bheinn Mhòr from the Abhainn Shira.

bashing on the walk out; although the road itself is peaceful, single track, and beautifully situated – in short, the envy of many paths!

A little over 500m up the road, a path turns off up the hillside along the edge of the Glenetive Forest plantations, approximating to the line of an historic route linking the heads of sea-lochs Etive and Creran. The path is through a shallow layer of peat overlying impermeable granite, and the result is that you'll almost certainly get your feet wet. The oily puddles and sulphurous stench liberated at many a footfall testify to the continuously waterlogged nature of this ground, and the oxygen-starved conditions in which vegetation slowly decomposes to build up peat over centuries. Higher up the going is drier, with much bracken (beware of ticks).

The path levels out at around 200m, above which the nose of Meall nan Gobhar rises in a series of craggy mounds which don't look particularly inviting. Pick the most obvious way up. The ascent is quite steep, but height is gained quickly. Higher up, exposed areas of slabby granite start appearing, giving a foretaste of things to come.

Loch Etive, the River Etive and Beinn Trilleachan from the west slopes of Stob Coir' an Albannaich.

A levelling is eventually reached which gives a stunning aerial view of the brilliant golden braids of the River Etive delta. Ben Starav is pretty impressive from here as well. Soon afterwards comes another levelling containing a lochan, after which a steep clamber past a solitary perched boulder 1.5m high leads up left of some granite slabs. The angle eases, and soon a narrow gully cuts into the ridge from the Loch Etive side.

Over another rise is a tiny lochan, dotted in summer with bright tufts of bog cotton. Beyond are two more sizeable boulders perched on the smooth Cruachan granite bedrock. These are further examples of glacial erratics: boulders of an often foreign geology dumped by the retreating ice. The larger is about 3m long, and delicately balanced. The Highlands are littered with such examples.

The ridge steadily becomes bald granite, reaching a cairned high point at 767m, marked on the OS 1:50 000 map as Trilleachan Slabs. There is a marked feeling of exposure here, and the views are superb, with distant Ben Cruachan particularly splendid down the ribbon of Loch Etive which, on a fine day, will be royal blue. A steep 70m clamber down a vegetated giant's staircase of granite leads to a heathery neck above a big gully plunging towards Loch Etive.

The promenade which follows is more or less unique in Britain. The granite is like smooth old bones except for patches of thin vegetation, mostly mosses. During the last glacial resurgence, ice

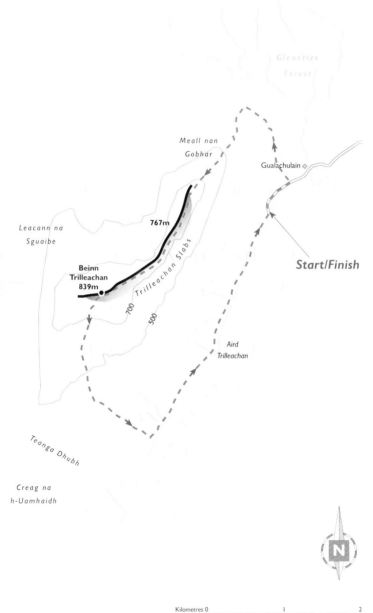

Glenetive
Forest

Meall nan
Gobhar

Gualachulain ◇

Leacann na
Sguaibe

767m

Trilleachan Slabs

Beinn
Trilleachan
839m ●

700

500

Start/Finish

Aird
Trilleachan

Teanga Dhubh

Creag na
h-Uamhaidh

N

Kilometres 0   1   2
Miles 0   1

probably covered Beinn Trilleachan, scouring it bare of the stony terraces and frost-shattered rocks which show that the higher peaks rose clear of the ice, and leaving calling-card erratics.

The final slow rise up to the great bald summit dome is enlivened by the plant-life. Here amongst the turf and short heath can be found the delicate blue harebell (*Campanula uniflora*), yellow four-petalled tormentil (*Potentilla erecta*), sheepsbit scabious (*Jasione Montana*) – like a little electric blue firework explosion – and the edible, bitter black fruit of crowberry (*Empitrum nigrum*).

The summit cairn is surrounded by ragged acres of granite pavement; fun for those who delight in the small-scale. In fact, there is no other Scottish mountain summit quite like this. The most satisfying finish to the walk is via the mountain's south-western slopes and the shores of Loch Etive. The ground south of the summit is very featureless however, and lies above some blind and nasty steep ground overlooking Loch Etive. If in doubt, it may be prudent to return by the same route.

Otherwise, head slightly west of due south onto a sloping, stream-seamed plateau of elevated bog, aiming for a vague corrie in Beinn Trilleachan's flank, which is more obvious from near the summit than from the map. The slopes of this depression give the easiest and most reliable descent to the loch, ending in deciduous woodland which is no real obstacle, but best negotiated at its narrowest point.

Above the loch shore is a faint path, which grows increasingly distinct as it leads along the beautifully wooded shore towards the day's starting point. This bit of the walk justifies the effort by itself. Here are beautiful mature specimens of alder (*Alnus glutinosa*), oak (*Quercus robur*), rowan (*Sorbus aucuparia*) – which with any luck will be sagging under fat fire-red berries – and holly (*Ilex aquifolium*).

The woodland remnants form extensive airy stands often inter-connected by more scattered trees. After about 1.5km, at a bracken-filled clearing, the path traverses close to a headland jutting into Loch Etive's ruffled waters. This is Aird Trilleachan, whose pebbly beach provides unforgettable views both down the loch and towards its head, with the upper Glen Etive peaks jostling in the distance. One of the best views of the Trilleachan Slabs is from here as well, the steepness of Beinn Trilleachan's flank and the loch's fjord-like character being fully apparent.

Beinn Trilleachan from Glen Etive.

Another 2km sees the last of the woodland fall behind, and the eternally squelching, sulphurous trench of the path leading back to the road-head.

WALK 20

BEINN SGULAIRD

Distance: 13km (8miles).

Ascent: 980m (3220ft).

Start/Finish: Car park near Elleric (GR035487), reached by minor road leaving the A828 at the head of Loch Creran.

Maps: OS Landranger 50 *Glen Orchy & surrounding area* or Pathfinder 319 *Head of Loch Etive.*

Terrain: A steep ascent with some rough rocky ground and some easy, bouldery scrambling.

Stalking Information: Glencreran Estate Ltd, tel. 01631 730312.

Gaelic names

> **Beinn Sgulaird** (bYn **sgoo**lart): Obscure, but possibly (big old) hat mountain.
> **Stob Gaibhre** (stob **gY**ra): Goat's peak.
> **An Grianan** (an**gree**-anan): The sunny spot.
> **Beinn Fhionnlaidh** (bYn **yoon**lY): Finlay,s mountain.
> **Glen Ure:** from gleann iubhair (glyown **yoo**-ar): yew-tree glen.

Beinn Sgulaird, though one of the less well-known peaks covered by this book, is a great little mountain and a fitting way to round off a selection of hillwalks in the Glen Coe and Lochaber area. It rises impressively above Glen Creran straight to a rough summit ridge in one unbroken craggy slope, and is even steeper above the lovely wooded defile of Glen Ure, which cleaves the mountain barrier separating Glen Creran from Glen Etive. Approached from Glen Ure it provides a scrambly outing of continual interest, ideally suited to a relaxed sunny day spent savouring shaggy views over shimmering lochs and rumbling streams.

It is possible to approach Beinn Sgulaird by the old cross-country route from Glen Etive, which shares the start of walk 19 before crossing the wet moorland above the head of Glen Ure. This however does no justice to the mountain: the views of it on the

Top: Stob Gaibhre and Beinn Sgulaird from near Glenure.

An Grianan from the Glen Ure track near Glenure.

approach are unflattering, and the walk-in is a good way to get fed up with the peak before even setting foot on it. The approach from Glen Creran, though rather remote from other walks described in this book, is infinitely finer.

Amid lovely deciduous woodland at the head of the short Glen Creran road is a sizeable car-park. Here a track turns off towards the farm of Glenure, soon crossing the River Creran, with Beinn Sgulaird's knobbly skyline looming high above sheep-cropped meadows and whitewashed farm buildings. Past the farm a bridge crosses the River Ure, beyond which a pleasant track strikes up Glen Ure towards the impressively rough and steep hillock of An Grianan.

Roughly 1.5km after the bridge, the track enters some delightful scrubby woodland where the river flows slackly over its bouldery bed. High above, a stream spills down a broad gully – almost a miniature corrie – from the obvious notch between the main body of Beinn Sgulaird and the prominent little peak of Stob Gaibhre.

In its lower reaches, this stream occupies a shallow, woodland-lined ravine, which acts as a marker for the ascent. Follow rough grassy slopes up to its left, winding through scattered birches as the ground becomes more rocky, following an increasingly well defined ridge. Keep an eye open for the small purple flowers of butterwort (*Pinguicula vulgaris*), with its insect-trapping leaves; the succulent, yellow flowered roseroot (*Rhodiola rosea*); and the spherical yellow flowers of the globeflower (*Trollius europeaus*). The ground is pretty steep but, taken at a steady pace, far from unpleasant; levelling out eventually on the rocky summit of Stob Gaibhre.

This is a superb viewpoint. Far below is the gorge-like defile of Glen Ure, clustered with a lush, broken carpet of mixed natural

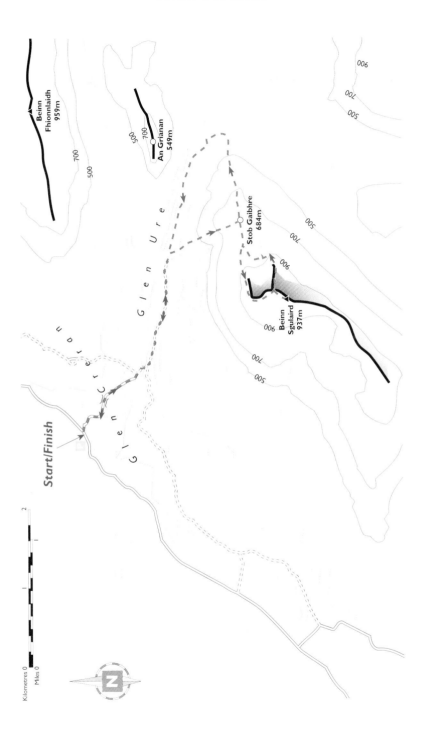

Beinn
Fhionnlaidh
959m

An Grianan
549m

Stob Gaibhre
684m

Beinn
Sgulaird
937m

Glen Ure

Glen Creran

Start/Finish

Kilometres 0
Miles 0

woodland. Above it rises the dome of Grianan, and above that loom the twin whalebacks of Beinn Fhionnlaidh. From here Beinn Sgulaird is a fine and steep symmetrical peak with large exposures of pink granite: slabby in its shallow, saucer-like eastern corrie, but more shattered on the almost identical enclosing ridges.

A short broad ridge is followed by an abrupt and steep descent to an idyllic lochan perched on the nick between the two peaks. Above rises Beinn Sgulaird's north eastern ridge. Broad and quite grassy at first, this is an utterly delightful and increasingly rocky mountain staircase, providing easy but hugely enjoyable scrambling over stacked granite boulders and small slabs on steeper sections between shelves of slabby outcrops and lawns of cropped turf.

Eventually the crest of the corrie's crescent-shaped summit ridge is reached. The summit, however, is still half a kilometre away over wild, hummocky ridges of short turf and cream to reddish granite outcrops reminiscent of parts of the Cairngorms and Arran. There is more scrambling to be enjoyed here: all avoidable, but who would want to avoid such fun? From the highest knoll on the crest of the eastern corrie, the mountain's spine bears off south-west, descending briefly before rising again to the bouldery 937m (3059ft) summit.

Many of the views from the summit are bettered by the peaks to the east around Loch Etive: to the south-west, Beinn Sgulaird begins to sprawl a bit, and the next mountain down, Creach Bheinn, is a pretty uninspiring heap. Beinn Trilleachan, seen from here across a vast heathery ice-scoured raised basin, is also a bit bloated, enlivened by the great areas of bare rock on its western flanks. On the other hand, the view across Loch Etive to Ben Cruachan is very fine indeed, as is that down Loch Creran. At the right time of day the sun shimmers mesmerisingly off the Firth of Lorn, where the limestone emerald of Lismore and a dozen smaller islands bask in the shelter of distant Mull.

The most satisfying descent is via the other of the two ridges bounding the eastern corrie, which is also quite rocky, but not as scrambly. Where its angle eases slightly, a descending traverse can be made across the corrie's often damp floor back to the lochan below

Stob Gaibhre. The easiest descent from here is via Stob Gaibhre's knolly eastern ridge until a way can be picked easily down the slopes above Glen Ure, joining a path which leads down above the glen's finely wooded gorge to the track, and hence back to the car park.

Globeflower and roseroot, on the slopes of Stob Gaibhre.

Index

Published by The Stationery Office and available from:

The Stationery Office Bookshops
71 Lothian Road, Edinburgh EH3 9AZ
(counter service only)
59-60 Holborn Viaduct, London EC1A 2FD
(Temporary location until mid-1998)
Fax 0171-831 1326
68-69 Bull Street, Birmingham B4 6AD
0121-236 9696 Fax 0121-236 9699
33 Wine Street, Bristol BS1 2BQ
0117-926 4306 Fax 0117-929 4515
9-21 Princess Street, Manchester M60 8AS
0161-834 7201 Fax 0161-833 0634
16 Arthur Street, Belfast BT1 4GD
01232 238451 Fax 01232 235401
The Stationery Office Oriel Bookshop
The Friary, Cardiff CF1 4AA
01222 395548 Fax 01222 384347

The Stationery Office publications are also available from:

The Publications Centre
(mail, telephone and fax orders only)
PO Box 276, London SW8 5DT
General enquiries 0171-873 0011
Telephone orders 0171-873 9090
Fax orders 0171-873 8200

Accredited Agents
(see Yellow Pages)

and through good booksellers

Printed in Scotland for The Stationery Office by CC No. 70343 50C 10/97 J12878